Friction Ridge Skin

Comparison and Identification
of Fingerprints

CRC SERIES IN
PRACTICAL ASPECTS OF CRIMINAL
AND FORENSIC INVESTIGATIONS

VERNON J. GEBERTH, BBA, MPS, FBINA *Series Editor*

Practical Homicide Investigation: Tactics, Procedures, and Forensic
  Techniques, Second Edition
Vernon J. Geberth

The Counter-Terrorism Handbook: Tactics, Procedures, and Techniques
Frank Bolz, Jr., Kenneth J. Dudonis, and David P. Schulz

Forensic Pathology
Dominick J. Di Maio and Vincent J. M. Di Maio

Interpretation of Bloodstain Evidence at Crime Scenes
William G. Eckert and Stewart H. James

Tire Imprint Evidence
Peter McDonald

Practical Drug Enforcement: Procedures and Administration
Michael D. Lyman

Practical Aspects of Rape Investigation: A Multidisciplinary Approach
Robert R. Hazelwood and Ann Wolbert Burgess

The Sexual Exploitation of Children: A Practical Guide to Assessment,
  Investigation, and Intervention
Seth L. Goldstein

Gunshot Wounds: Practical Aspects of Firearms, Ballistics, and
  Forensic Techniques
Vincent J. M. Di Maio

Friction Ridge Skin: Comparison and Identification of Fingerprints
James F. Cowger

Footwear Impression Evidence
William J. Bodziak

Practical Aspects of Kinesic Interview and Interrogation Techniques
Stan Walters

Practical Fire and Arson Investigation
John J. O'Connor

A Practical Methodology of Forensic Photography
David R. Redsicker

Practical Gambling Investigation Techniques
Kevin B. Kinnee

Practical Aspects of Interview and Interrogation
David E. Zulawski and Douglas E. Wicklander

Practical Investigation Techniques
Kevin B. Kinnee

Friction Ridge Skin

Comparison and Identification
of Fingerprints

James F. Cowger

Identification Officer
Contra Costa County Sheriff–Coroner's Department
Martinez, California

CRC Press
Boca Raton Boston New York Washington London

Library of Congress Cataloging-in-Publication Data

Cowger, James F.
    Friction ridge skin : comparison and identification of fingerprints / James F. Cowger.
        p. cm.
    Originally published: New York : Elsevier, 1983. (Elsevier series in practical aspects
of criminal and forensic investigations)
    Includes bibliographical references and index.
    ISBN 0-8493-9502-X
      1. Fingerprints. 2. Criminals—Identification. I. Title. II. Series: Elsevier series in
practical aspects of criminal and forensic investigations.
HV6074.C64 1993
363.2'58—dc20   93-24980
                                                                     CIP

Visit the CRC Press Web site at www.crcpress.com

© 1983 by Elsevier Science Publishing Co. Inc.
© 1993 by CRC Press LLC

No claim to original U.S. Government works
International Standard Book Number 0-8493-9502-X
Library of Congress Card Number   93-24980
Printed in the United States of America   11 12 13 14 15
Printed on acid-free paper

This book is dedicated to
the memory of my friend and teacher,
Lester S. Deicke,
who taught me that things are seldom
as simple as they first appear.

Contents

Preface

There are many books available that address the subject of personal identification. There are a number of other books that include the subject as a part of a general discussion of forensic sciences. For the most part these expositions treat the practice as a technicians task, governed by set rules and fixed techniques. Due to the nature of the field, advancements are few and are usually either mere adjustments of old techniques or accidental discoveries in other fields.

I do not present this book to expose an important new discovery in tool or technique, although some with experience in this area may find something new to them. My purpose in this book is to approach the field in which I toil from a different perspective. Avoided will be rules that are applied only when it is convenient, rules honored in statement but not in practice. Traditional practices and techniques that are no longer valid are eschewed. It is recognized that, when well and properly done, the practice of this discipline requires knowledge, understanding, and the ability to define a problem and find a solution.

All of this can be summed up in a simple statement: *Friction ridge comparison is a forensic science.*

For those first encountering this subject, it is my hope that this book will generate an appreciation of the science sufficient to carry them beyond the confines of its pages. For experienced criminalists it is my intention that this book serve as a bridge to close the gap between them and identification specialists. Most of all, however, I desire experienced specialists in this field to find, among the technical information, food for thought.

JAMES F. COWGER

Acknowledgments

I must acknowledge the assistance of my spouse and child who allowed me to ignore them for weeks on end and my employer, the Contra Costa County Sheriff–Coroner's Department, for allowing me to use their files for resource material. Contributors of other material and illustrations are credited in the text.

Introduction

1

Covering the palmar surfaces of the hands and the plantar surfaces of the feet is friction ridged skin (Figure 1.1). Of all the attributes of humankind, this friction skin is the only one that is currently capable of individualization to the extent that it is possible, within practical limits, to say that no two people are alike. That such is the case is accepted today as fact even by those who have no knowledge of how the friction skin of two individuals differ.

Friction ridges form on the hands and feet of a fetus before birth; barring injury (Figure 1.2), their form does not change during life. These ridges are not continuous parallel lines, but have endings and *bifurcations* (points where a ridge divides into two ridges). A ridge may be quite short and may be so short as to appear as a dot. It is the orientation, location, and interrelationship of these features in the coursing of the friction ridges that makes it possible to determine whether two prints were made by the same individual.

That the arrangement of these minutiae is sufficiently different on each finger, palm, toe, and sole that every individual can be considered unique has been validated by decades of work by thousands of examiners. There has yet to be reported an instance of two prints being so similar that their donors could not be differentiated. This does not prove that no two such prints will *ever* be found; it does, however, indicate that the probability of such an occurrence is infinitesimally small, and can be considered nonexistent for practical purposes.

Although many decades of experience by dedicated workers may seem sufficient to support the individuality of friction skin, many have attempted to demonstrate its individuality using calculations of probability. The first such calculation was published in the landmark

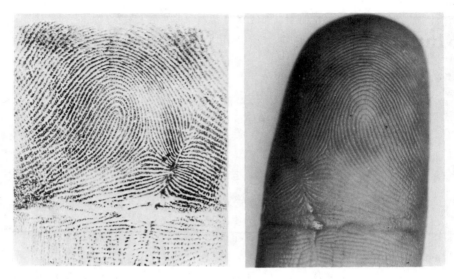

Figure 1.1 An inked fingerprint and the finger that made it.

treatise *Finger Prints* (Galton, 1892) and stated that the probability of duplication of an entire fingerprint was .25. More recently, the probability of the occurrence of but a portion of a fingerprint has been calculated to be 10^{-20} (Osterburg et al., 1977). The probability of duplication, based on this figure, is substantially greater given the extent of each individual fingerprint and the fact that almost everyone has 10 fingers. Thus, the mathematical and empirical (experiential) data are more than adequate to provide a *very* sound basis for the use of friction skin prints as a means of positive, certain identification.

A number of researchers have shown that the *patterns* in friction ridged skin are affected by genetic factors (Srivastava, 1965; Mukherjee, 1966; Holt, 1968). These patterns are the *general* flows of the friction ridges. There is as yet no evidence that the arrangement of the minutiae (ending ridges, bifurcating ridges, etc.) is in any way genetically influenced. Even in cases of very close kinship, such as identical (monozygotic) twins the prints of the individuals are still easily distinguished by comparison of the minutiae, although the pattern types may be quite similar. Prenatal illness, however, can affect fingerprints, causing what is known as dissociation of the ridges: disrupted ridge flows and dotted, rather than continuous, ridges (Figure 1.3).

Friction ridged skin is a highly specialized organ and differs from the skin on the rest of the body in more than simply its ridged appearance. It has no hair follicles and, thus, no apocrine or sebaceous glands. These papillary ridges are orderly rows of eccrine (sweat)

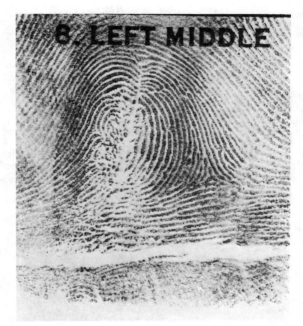

Figure 1.2 The effects of scarring.

glands which are distributed in excess of 400/cm^2; the average distribution over the rest of the skin surface averages but 130/cm^2. Friction ridged skin is also thicker than other skin and contains more nerve endings than other parts of the body (Montagna, 1956).

Friction ridges for traction, thicker skin for protection from injury, no sebaceous glands to secrete waxy, oily sebum, no hair to come between the skin and what is grasped or trod, and a heightened sense of touch makes friction skin ideal as a covering for palms and soles. Fortunately, the arrangement of the friction ridges also makes it ideal as a means of determining identity.

Although humans were undoubtedly long aware of the existence of the friction ridges on their hands and feet, the earliest written reference to friction skin is a paper by Dr. Nehemiah Grew (1684) delivered to the Royal Society in London. In the paper Grew reported on the patterning of the fingers and palms, and commented on the arrangement of the sweat pores along the ridges. He did not deal with the individuality of friction skin and it seems certain that he did not consider it. Still, the paper marked the beginning of the scientific consideration of friction skin.

Close behind Grew came Bidloo (1685) and Malpighi (1686) with additional descriptions of the morphology of friction skin. Malpighi is perhaps the more important because, while Bidloo published a de-

Figure 1.3 Fingerprint showing the appearance of dissociated ridges.

tailed description of the skin covering the fingers, Malpighi investigated the function of friction skin as a tactile organ and as a means of providing traction for walking and grasping.

In 1788 the first published reference to the potential uniqueness of friction skin appeared in an atlas of medical illustrations by J.C.A. Mayer, who wrote:

> Although the arrangement of skin ridges is never duplicated in two persons, nevertheless the similarities are clearer among some individuals. In others the differences are marked, yet in spite of their peculiarities of arrangement all have a certain likeness (Mayer, 1788).

While it is apparent that Mayer's intent was to point out that prints are similar (perhaps in the same manner that people all have the same number and types of bones) he must be credited with being the first to record that prints are different.

In a thesis about the physiological processes of the skin, Johannes Purkinje (1823) devised the first systematic classification of fingerprint patterns while a university professor in Bohemia. The thesis did not, however, address individuality. The classification he devised utilized nine categories of pattern, each defined quite specifically. That subsequent investigators did not continue or build upon Purkinje's classification system may be an indication that his role has been overstated in the past.

The first published mention of the possibility of using friction ridged skin as a means of identification appeared as a note in the journal *Nature* (Faulds, 1880). The author, a doctor serving in a medical mission in Japan, stated much later that his interest was initially aroused when he noticed impressions of fingerprints in Japanese pottery. That his investigation of friction skin was thorough is illustrated by the fact that his Japanese students even went so far as to destroy the skin on their fingers by abrasion, acid, and other methods, so that they could determine if the prints would be changed when their fingers healed.

Faulds' concept, as published, was that fingerprints would be primarily useful as a technique for investigation of evidence left at scenes of crimes. His article describes two instances in which he used such evidence in Japan:

> I have already met with two practical cases in my experience, and was able to use such fingerprints as necessary evidence. In one case someone had left greasy fingerprints on a drinking glass. . . . In the other case, the sooty fingerprints left by a person climbing over a white wall were of great value as exonerating evidence. (Faulds, 1880)

Shortly after the appearance of Faulds' first publication, Sir William Herschel wrote to *Nature* claiming to have discovered the individuality of friction skin long before Faulds. Herschel wrote that he had been using fringerprints for more than 20 years as a colonial official in the Hooghly district in India. He stated further that he had introduced the practice in several government departments in 1877. He also claimed that his experience over those years without finding changes in fingerprints proved the utility of the scheme.

A debate ensued in various journals between Faulds and Herschel regarding who should receive credit for first discovering the individuality of fingerprints and their potential usefulness in personal identification.

It was while researching this controversy, for a lecture to the Royal Institute on the Bertillon system of identification (discussed later in this chapter), that Sir Francis Galton first became interested in fingerprints. Galton had been aware of the subject since about 1880 but did not begin his investigation until 1888. The result of his study was the aforementioned book, *Finger Prints* (Galton, 1892). In this book, Galton considered virtually every aspect of friction skin including history, morphology, inheritance, individuality, permanence, methods of printing, and potential usefulness. Though most of the data he used are out of date, and the book itself out of print, *Finger Prints* is a landmark treatise marking the beginning of the modern use of the prints of friction skin as a means of identification.

In Argentina, Dr. Juan Vucetich instituted the use of "icnofalangometrica" in the La Plata police department in 1891. It is interesting that Vucetich's use of fingerprints predated the publication of Galton's book; he was undoubtably influenced by the writing of Faulds and Herschel. The classification devised by Vucetich is still in use, with local modifications and extensions, in most Spanish-speaking countries.

Besides Faulds, Herschel, and Galton, another British civil servant who figures prominently in the history of the use of fingerprints is Sir Edward Richard Henry. Henry was the Inspector General of Police in Bengal, India and visited Galton in 1893. As a result of that visit he returned to India to institute the use of fingerprints as an aid to identification on a national level. Henry's classification system, for which he is best known, was devised between 1894 and 1897 with the assistance of two Indian civil servants. In 1897, India officially discarded the use of Bertillonage in favor of the use of fingerprints and the Henry classification system. In 1901, as the Assistant Commissioner in charge of criminal identification at New Scotland Yard, Henry began the use of fingerprints as an adjunct to the use of Bertillonage.

Bertillonage (McLaughery, 1896), named after its originator, French criminologist Alphonse Bertillon, was an identification system much in use in the latter part of the 19th and the very early 20th centuries. In this system individuals were subjected to measurement of various body parts and minute description (the "portrait parle"), (Figure 1.4). The data thus collected were arranged into a formula and filed. The measurements and description of the individual, although performed under rigorous guidelines, were subject to much operator error due to their interpretive nature. As the files for the system grew, first photographs and then fingerprints were added to improve its accuracy.

Perhaps because fingerprints were easier to take, did not depend on the judgment of some person at some other time and place, and were not affected by aging or purposeful changes of appearance, fingerprints gradually replaced Bertillonage as the preferred method of personal identification. In the United States, the use of Bertillonage began a rapid decline in 1903 when two prisoners in the penitentiary at Ft. Leavenworth, Kansas, were found to be indistinguishable on the basis of photographs and Bertillon measurements. In Europe, however, Bertillonage was not abandoned until after the death of Alphonse Bertillon in 1914.

The use of friction skin prints is usually considered to have two distinct functions. The first is *record keeping* where a complete set of fingerprints of an individual is used to determine the true identity of that individual. The second in *criminal matters* to implicate an individual as possibly responsible for the criminal activity. In fact,

MEASURING THE LENGTH OF LEFT FOOT (a)

Figure 1.4 One of the many measurements of the anthropometrical identification system of Bertillon.

both of these applications are but two sides of the same coin. The only difference is that in record keeping the worker usually has a greater amount of material with which to work and that material is prepared for that specific purpose. In crime investigation, some of the material that is used was not made purposely and is likely to consist of incomplete and poorly recorded friction skin prints made on glass, paper, walls, weapons, and the like. Although there may be a vast difference in the degree of difficulty of the tasks at times, the process of identifying an individual by the use of the characteristics of the friction skin is, in both cases, the same.

Taking Inked Prints

2

Inked prints can be considered a general term to describe prints of friction skin that are purposely made by any appropriate technique and for any purpose. While it is generally true that such prints could be more descriptively called *known* or *exemplar* prints, it does happen on occasion that such prints constitute the unknown or questioned print, the identity of the donor of which is to be sought.

There have been many methods and materials devised for the purpose of preparing exemplar prints, all of which have been touted as producing the best possible prints. Some are devised to be clean, some quick, some to produce the finest detail. All, at least for their inventors, do serve their purpose. Whether the method used involves photographic paper, powder and adhesive "lifting," chemical development, or just plain ink, the point of the process is to produce legible prints that are suitable for classification and comparison.

The most common method of recording prints of friction skin is with ink. Other techniques may be necessary in isolated circumstances but, as a general rule, ink serves well because it is easy to use and produces prints of good detail and high contrast. Subjects to be printed are usually living and, unless uncooperative, the process of printing is rather straightforward. There are, of course, circumstances that may require special techniques. Where the subject to be printed is deceased, for instance, extraordinary measures must occasionally be taken to secure legible prints.

The extent of the printing to be done is determined by the circumstances of the particular case. If an individual is being printed to confirm or establish identity, to determine if the subject has a prior criminal record, then it is unlikely that it will be necessary to do more than take an ordinary set of fingerprints (Figure 2.1). If the individual being printed is suspected of activity of a type that may have left prints or impressions of friction skin at a crime scene or on an object associated with a crime, then it may be necessary to also take palm prints. In certain circumstances it may be necessary to produce a set of *major criminal* prints—a record of *all* of the friction skin covering the palms and fingers. Some cases may even require toe and sole prints to be made.

The goal that is to be addressed in any situation is to obtain a recording of the friction ridge skin that is of adequate quality for the comparisons that are subsequently to be made. Ideally, such prints will have good contrast, clear detail, and be complete. The methods that are available for making such prints are numerous, limited only by imagination and the availability of materials. The following discussion will address some of these methods.

Prints of the Living

Fingerprints

Prints of the living are usually made quite easily. This is generally accomplished by applying a thin coat of ink to the friction ridges of the finger or palm and then pressing it on a piece of paper. Because of the difference in elevation between the ridges and valleys of the friction skin, it will act much like a rubber stamp and leave a print that is a recording of the detail of the friction ridges.

Little equipment is necessary to take good quality exemplar prints (Figure 2.2): an ink brayer (roller), an inking plate of glass or smooth metal, the necessary forms (fingerprint and palm prints cards) or other appropriate paper stock for recording the prints, and an oil-based ink sufficiently viscous so as not to be readily absorbed into the paper stock which would cause the prints to be blurry.

First, a thin coat of ink is rolled out on the ink plate. This coat of ink should appear black, not gray, and should not look "wet." If the ink on the plate looks gray the resultant prints will be light, perhaps lacking sufficient contrast for effective classification and comparison. If the coat of ink looks shiny and wet the likely result will be prints that are blurred and smudged. Even if the prints look fine when first made, if there is too much ink present they can be smudged with subsequent handling, reducing their usefulness.

After the proper amount of ink has been rolled onto the plate, the next step is to ink the fingers. As much as possible, the fingers should be clean and dry. Dirt or debris on the skin can prevent good contact of the skin to the ink and to the card, or it may itself print causing

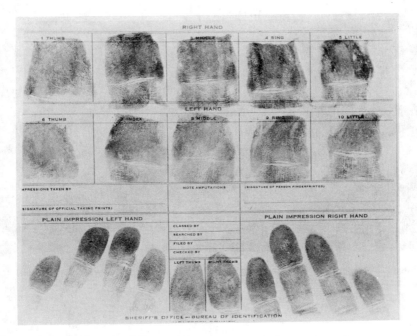

Figure 2.1 A complete set of fingerprints.

poor prints. If the skin is too damp it will be difficult to produce good prints because the excess moisture can keep the ridges from being properly inked. Two key factors in securing good prints are *control* and *pressure.*

Friction skin courses around a finger that is usually conical in shape. In order to obtain a complete print of the friction ridges, the finger must be rolled. Thus, if sufficient control of the digit is not exercised it is likely that the print will be incomplete or smudged or both. Too much or too little pressure can also be a cause of poor prints, regardless of the amount of control exercised, because it can cause improper ink transfer or excessive distortion (stretching of the skin).

In inking the finger and making the print the hand should be grasped firmly in such a manner that the finger being printed is extended and the other fingers are out of the way. The hand is rotated so that the side of the finger can be placed on the ink plate. While one hand is grasping the hand of the subject the other hand is holding the end of the finger being printed to keep it from slipping and to apply light pressure. The finger is then rotated on the ink plate until

Figure 2.2 A common fingerprinting setup showing the inking plate, cardholder, and ink brayer.

the other side of the finger is on the plate (Figure 2.3a). The rotation should encompass approximately 180 degrees. The finger should then be lifted from the plate and rolled in the appropriate place on the card in the same manner as it was inked (Figure 2.3b).

It is recommended that the direction of the roll of the digit be toward the body for the thumbs and away from the body for the fingers. That is, when the thumb is placed on the ink plate and the card the direction of rotation should take it toward the body of the person being printed; the fingers should rotate away from the subject's body. The reason for this has to do with the construction of the forearm and the placement of the thumb and fingers with respect to radial bone. As a practical matter the fingers and thumb are rolled from a position of stress to a more relaxed position, reducing the chance of slippage on either the ink plate or the card. In practice it is of little consequence whether the digits are rolled in the prescribed direction or not. The goal is to produce a set of clear, complete prints. If the person taking the prints is more comfortable rolling the fingers and thumbs in the same direction and produces a good set of prints doing so, then the direction of rotation does not matter.

There are a number of variables that, if not controlled, can interfere with producing clear prints. Inking, control of the digit, and pressure have already been mentioned. A variable not within the control of the printer is the shape of the finger. If the fingers were cylindrical it would be relatively easy to get prints that were clear and unsmudged

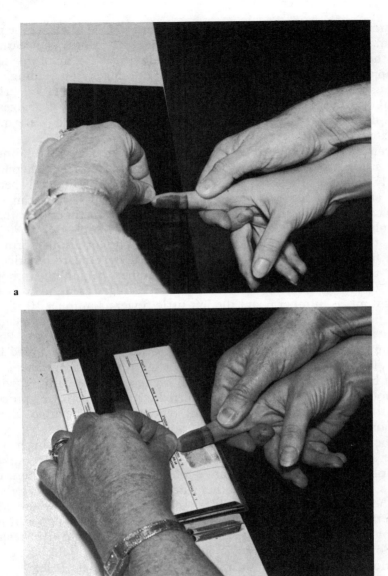

Figure 2.3 a. Inking a finger. The finger must be well controlled and rolled fully. **b.** Printing a finger. Done in the same manner as inking.

from top to bottom. However, since the digits are usually conical, different parts will rotate at different speeds when rolled on the ink plate and the card. The result of this is usually smudged, unclear ridges at the tip of the print. This can be largely overcome if the printer bears in mind that skin is usually quite flexible, and its ability to stretch and compress can help to make it possible to overcome this natural tendency to smudge. With practice the printer can learn to roll the digit as if it is indeed a cone with its tip at the tip of the digit. By applying just enough pressure to keep the ridges from sliding, and taking advantage of the stretching ability of the skin, good prints should result. Excess ink can act as a lubricant allowing the ridges to slide despite the best efforts of the printer in this regard. Care must be exercised in this area.

Even with proper inking, the print may be smudged by sliding if the card or paper stock being used has too slick a surface. Therefore, highly coated paper should be avoided. On the other hand, paper or card stock that has a surface that is too rough or fibrous can also detract from the clarity of the prints by making them appear fuzzy and blurred.

A standard fingerprint card has 10 blocks, one for a rolled print of each finger. The blocks are numbered and it is standard practice to refer to each finger by its appropriate number: beginning from the right thumb as number 1 to the right little finger as number 5; the left thumb as number 6 and the left little finger as number 10. There is also additional space at the bottom of the card for what are called *plain impressions* (see Figure 2.1). These have two purposes. First, they provide a check on the sequence of the individually rolled fingers. The four fingers of each hand, being printed simultaneously, must be in their proper order. Second, because they are printed without rolling, there is less distortion introduced in the printing process and, if the entire pattern of the print appears, a more accurate classification can be determined.

When inking fingers, care should be taken to not ink a finger on a place where another finger was inked. If the plate was properly inked, the inking of a finger will remove most or all of the ink where the ridges contact the plate. If another finger is inked on that place there will be no ink placed on the ridges of the second finger where they cross the print left by the first finger. The result will be a poor, if not completely useless, print. It has even happened that the print resulting from such poor practice will appear to be good but will be a combination of both prints, causing the print to be misclassified and, perhaps, preventing identification.

Palm Prints

Palm prints are prepared in a manner similar to that for fingerprints. A thin coating of ink is applied to the ridges and the palm is then pressed to a card or sheet of paper to record the ridges. The palm is not inked from the ink plate, however, but is inked with the roller (Figure 2.4). The same requirements of cleanliness and ink quality

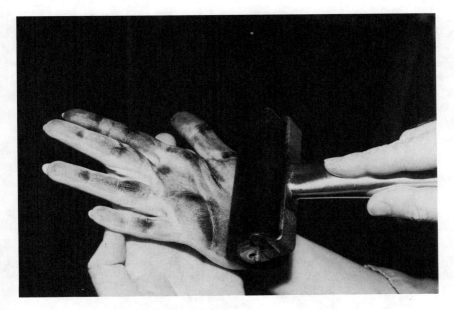

Figure 2.4 Inking a palm using the ink brayer.

and quantity that apply to fingerprints also apply to palm prints. It is somewhat more difficult to judge the amount of ink on the usually black rubber roller than on a glass or shiny metal plate; but if the ink on the plate appears right, the ink on the roller should also be of the right quantity.

Just as the fingers are not cylindrical, the palms are not flat. The topography of the palm is, in fact, quite complex. Fortunately, however, the hand is usually flexible enough to allow good prints to be made without great difficulty. If the hand were inked and just placed flat on a piece of paper, most of the palm would be printed, but not all. The areas usually missed by such technique are the center of the palm, a substantial portion just below the fingers and some of the region between the thumb and the fingers (Figure 2.5). If the palm being printed has a large degree of relief a great deal of it may not print at all if precautions are not taken.

A good technique for making palm prints that are quite complete is very simple. After inking the palm from the wrist to the tips of the fingers with the roller, ensuring that it is completely inked, the hand is inspected for areas of over-inking. Because it will be necessary to make a number of passes with the roller there may be areas that are over-inked. If any areas are over-inked, the excess ink can be removed by dabbing with a piece of paper or a towel and re-inked if necessary.

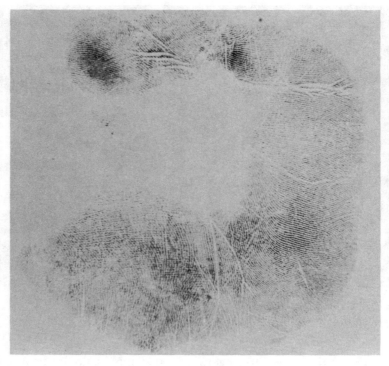

Figure 2.5 An incompletely printed palm print.

The edges of the roller may leave darker lines across the palm, but unless the ink has filled in the valleys between the ridges, these lines seldom cause problems.

The hand being printed is then firmly grasped at the wrist with one hand. The printer then uses his or her other hand to pull back and slightly separate the subject's fingers while pressing into the center of the back of the hand with the thumb. This helps to flatten the palm and open up much of the folds and creases that are commonly present in palms. The hand being printed is then placed on the card or paper, wrist first, and lowered into full contact, at which point the fingers are released (Figure 2.6a). Then, while still holding the wrist to prevent movement, the hand which had been holding the fingers is used to press firmly on the fingers of the hand being printed just above the palm and then in the center of the palm (Figure 2.6b). The last step, while still maintaining good control, is to use both hands to rotate the printed hand to the outside, away from the subject's

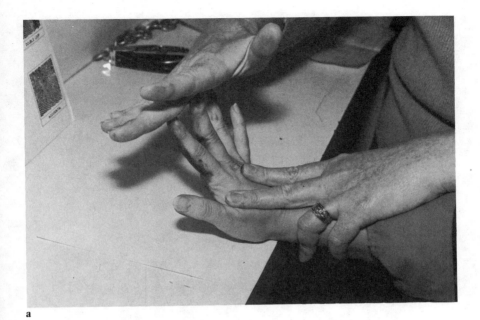

a

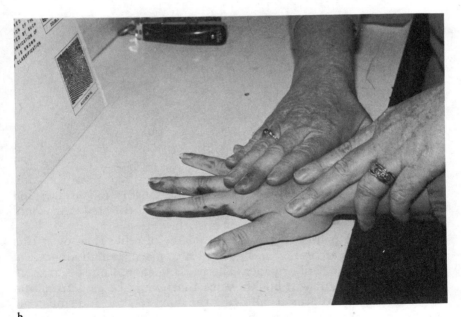

b

Figure 2.6 a. Applying the inked palm to the card. **b.** The hand is pressed to flatten the palm on the card.

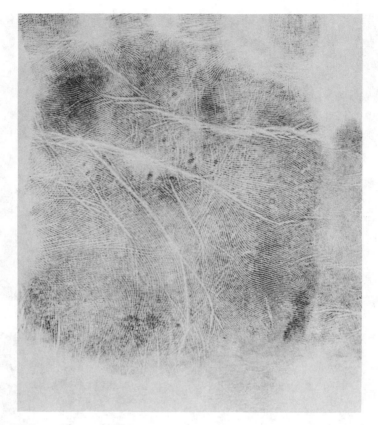

Figure 2.7 A complete palm print.

body, until it is approximately vertical and then lift it from the card. This rotation is desirable because palms, like fingers, have ridges and occasionally even patterning that extends beyond the area that would be printed by just pressing it flat against the card.

Because some palms have a greater degree of relief than even this technique can overcome, it is a good idea to place a small amount of padding under the card or paper. The padding should not be so thick or soft that the card will buckle since that would be as detrimental to producing a good print as allowing the hand to slide and smear the print or over or under inking the palm. Paper towels or a folded cloth about ¼ in. thick is usually adequate to provide the necessary flexibility without allowing the card to buckle. Figure 2.7 shows a more complete print of the same palm in Figure 2.5.

There are devices available which are intended to make taking palm prints quick and easy. These consist principally of large rollers to which the card is attached. The inked palm is then placed on the card and then drawn back or pushed forward causing the card and roller to rotate. This is a modernized version of an old practice of using a large can and rolling it across a table with a card between it and the palm. These devices can work quite well. However, because of the amount of motion involved, a good deal of practice and a co-operative subject are usually necessary to produce an acceptable print. These devices also do not allow printing the side of the palm without a second operation.

Other Devices and Materials for Recording Prints

Devices and materials devised to make taking prints easier and to control the variables involved in the printing process abound. Among these are the "inkless" printing systems, which are of two basic types. One uses a chemical process in which a nearly colorless chemical is placed on the finger or palm which is then printed to the card. Another chemical, with which the paper has been impregnated causes the print to darken sufficiently for classification and comparison. The other process, which does not require treated paper, has the developing agent in a spray can. After the finger is printed using the first chemical agent, the paper or card is sprayed with the developing agent and the prints darken.

These chemical systems generally produce prints which are of lower contrast than prints made with ordinary fingerprint ink and, unless made on paper that has a very smooth surface, lack the very find definition that is possible with ink. This is caused by the very liquid chemicals which are absorbed into the paper instead of remaining on the surface as does the oil-base ink. Also, unless very carefully prepared, prints made by this method can blur over a period of time as excess chemical migrates through the paper. This is not to say that these chemical systems are necessarily poor or should not be used. They have a definite value because they are relatively clean for both the operator and the subject. The fact that they will not get ink all over their hands is at times an advantage when the subject is being printed voluntarily. The materials are also easier to carry out to the field because it is not necessary to contend with inking plates, rollers, and tubes of ink that may leak. With these systems it is also not necessary to carry cleaners and large quantities of toweling for cleaning the subject's hands.

A device that allows inked prints to be made without getting ink on the subject's hands consists of a very thin, pliable membrane with a very thin coat of very tacky ink on one side. The membrane is held in a cardboard mount similar to a photo slide mount. The inked side

Figure 2.8 A fingerprint made with a membrane type printing device.

of the membrane is placed against the card and the finger or palm is pressed against it. Because of the thinness and pliability of the membrane the ridges will print through. The subject's hands remain clean and the materials are easily carried, but because of the necessary thinness of the ink film a membrane is quite limited in the number of acceptable prints it will produce. Figure 2.8 shows a print made with this material. The print was made with a device that had been used a number of times allowing the texture of the film to become apparent.

Other types of device that attempt, and succeed to an extent, to control variables are also available. The most controllable of the variables is the application of the proper film of ink to the ridges. One such device replaces the traditional ink roller and plate with an electrically driven, soft rubber pillow (Figure 2.9). A thin, even coating of ink is maintained on the pillow as it is rotated in response to touching it with the finger. The pillow is soft enough that it is not necessary to roll the finger on the ink as light pressure will cause the pillow almost to surround the finger. On most of these devices the pillow is attached to a handle and can be removed for inking palms if desired. This device is quite successful in accomplishing its purpose and its only apparent drawback is that it is impractical for field use.

A material that accomplishes the same purpose as the electrically operated inking device consists of a thin piece of plastic or acetate material to which a thin coat of ink has been applied. This material

Figure 2.9 A common type of electric inking device.

simply replaces the roller, plate, and tube of ink. It is used just as an inked plate would be used for inking the fingers. While a number of sets of prints can be made with a single sheet of this material, the number is certainly limited. However, the material is easily carried in a pocket or notebook and, with a little care, can produce very good prints.

There are a number of seldom used methods of obtaining prints of friction skin which, if nothing else, are illustrative of the ingenuity of those working in the field of identification. One of the more interesting techniques involves the use of photographic materials. Easily done, the printer carefully swabs photographic developer on the finger or palm and then prints onto fogged photographic paper. Because this is done in a lit room, the developer will eventually develop the paper where the ridges have contacted it. The print is then fixed in a "hypo" solution, washed, and dried. It is possible to produce a print of very fine detail in this way. The developer needs to be highly concentrated since only a small amount is to be transferred to the paper.

Using the same materials, with one addition, it is possible to produce a negative print—a white print with a black background. Instead of treating the ridges with developer, they are coated with any convenient oily substance (e.g., light machine oil) and printed to the photographic paper. The paper is developed and fixed normally. The oily substance will prevent the developer from being absorbed into and developing the paper where the ridges contacted it. If the paper is substituted by a negative material then the result will be a photographic negative that can be used to make enlargements of excellent quality.

Another method of making prints uses materials normally used to develop latent prints. Here the fingers or palms are "dusted" with fingerprint powder and the powder lifted with an adhesive material. If the lifting material is transparent and it is placed on an opaque backing, the print will be reversed, left to right, from a normally made print. It is advisable, therefore, to use a transparent backing for prints made this way and mark them so that there will be no confusion as to from which side they should be viewed. There are, however, opaque adhesive materials which are available and if these are used the prints obtained will be correctly oriented and no confusion as to orientation can result.

Regardless of the method of printing that is selected, the printer should practice it until it is certain that the best possible prints will result. A technique that produces excellent results for one user may produce poor results for another who is unfamiliar with its use. It is, of course, better to make an adequate set of prints with a familiar technique than to make a poor set with a more "sophisticated" but unfamiliar technique.

Major Criminal Prints

Although a properly taken set of finger and palm prints will serve most purposes, it is sometimes necessary to carry the printing process even farther. A set of *major criminal* prints is a recording of *all* of the friction ridged skin that covers the hands. Regularly prepared finger and palm prints do not record the ridges at the very tips of the fingers, usually not the middle joints of the fingers and certainly not their sides. Major criminal prints do record these areas. It may seem, at first thought, that such a set of prints would be useful in any case. That may be true; however, the time involved in preparing such an extensive set of prints is such that they are usually prepared only when it is known that the prints to which the subject's prints are to be compared were made by areas not ordinarily printed. It may also be believed that an individual will, in the future, engage in such criminal activity that a set of major criminal prints will become useful.

Preparation of these extensive prints begins with a very good set of finger and palm prints being made. When making the palm prints, care should be taken to avoid leaving any blank areas, paying particular attention to the areas of the palm just below the fingers and between the thumb and the fingers. On the margins of the palm, at the wrist and the ulnar or outside of the hand, the printing should extend all the way to the point where the friction ridges cease and the nonfriction ridged skin begins. It is advisable to go beyond this border, in fact, in order to ensure that the palm is completely printed. If necessary, additional prints should be made, paying particular attention to areas that may have been incompletely recorded or are otherwise questionable.

Recording all of the friction ridges on the fingers and thumbs is somewhat more difficult than printing the palms. First, each digit is inked and fully rolled on the paper from its base at the palm to its tip (Figure 2.10a). Inking the finger for this operation may, on some individuals, be difficult and it may be necessary to utilize an inking method other than the ink plate or roller. Here, the inking films may be used to advantage, or devices designed to assist in printing the dead may be utilized. Rolling the fingers in this manner may not be possible with the card holder that is used for ordinary fingerprinting and, because the other fingers may not have sufficient flexibility to be held out of the way, a table edge or counter of even thickness may present an impediment to obtaining good prints. To overcome this problem, the author has used an ordinary clipboard which is shortened so that a standard 8 in. × 8 in. card, when held by the clip, extends just to the edge. The clipboard can be clamped to a table or counter with its edge protruding a few inches. This provides a solid, very thin support with minimal interference.

After the initial rolled print of the entire digit, and as many additional prints as necessary to ensure the best possible recording, the sides of the fingers are again printed. Reinked, if necessary, the finger is placed on one side and raised in an arc until the tip of the finger is in contact with the paper (Figure 2.10b). This is done for both sides of the finger. Then the tip of the finger is printed by placing the finger on its side and rolling the finger, on its tip, to the other side. Lastly, the finger is placed flat on the paper and raised up until it is vertical to the paper. The order in which the various operations are done is, certainly, a matter of preference, but each print should be properly identified as to its appropriate digit. Figure 2.11a, b shows a set of prints for a fully printed finger.

In this manner it is possible to print all of the friction skin of a hand. Doing this does require a great deal of care and a substantial amount of practice in order to get the best possible prints with a minimal amount of reprinting. Because of the stresses that are usually involved in manipulating a person's hand through the printing pro-

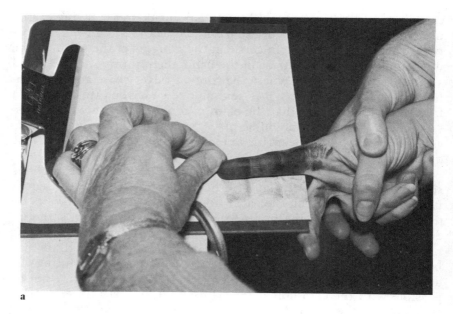

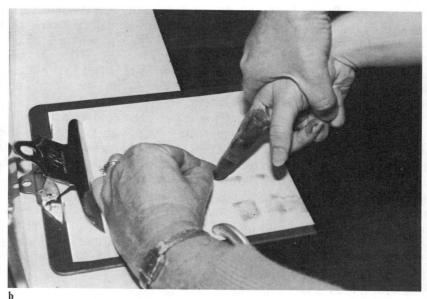

Figure 2.10 a. Rolling a finger for a "major criminal set". **b.** Printing the side of a finger.

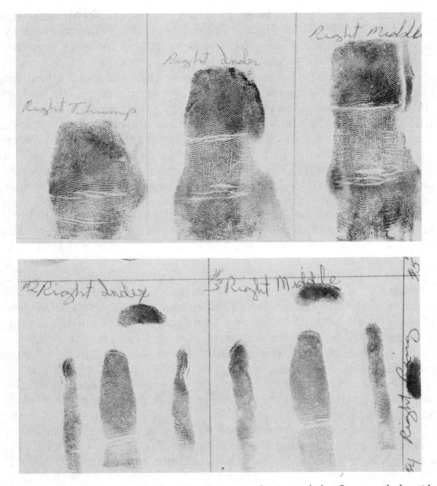

Figure 2.11 A finger completely printed to record joints of the finger and the side and tip.

cess it is advisable for each individual to develop a personal technique; the comfort and ease of the person taking the prints is as important to good results as the comfort of the subject.

Printing Problem Subjects

Obtaining prints of some individuals present particular problems, where because of injury or disease the usual methods will simply not serve. Such problems can almost always be overcome with patience and imagination. Persons to be printed at times will have additional digits, webbed or joined fingers, suffer from arthritis or rheumatism, have palsy, or simply have skin with so little relief that even the thinnest layer of ink seems to fill the ridges.

In situations where the subject has more than the usual allotment of digits—*polydactyly*—the additional digit is printed on the back of the fingerprint card if the printing is simply a matter of personal identification. Such additional digits are usually fingers and the one on the outside of the hand is considered "extra" for the purposes of printing and classification. If the additional digit is on the thumb side of the hand, again the outermost digit is considered to be supernumerary and is printed separately. If the prints are being made for the purpose of comparing them with prints from a crime scene, for instance, then whatever measures necessary to secure a clear set of prints should be taken and conventions regarding the placement of the fingers on the card may not need to be followed so long as the order of the digits is properly indicated.

Where fingers are "webbed" or joined, a congenital defect called *syndactyly*, it may not be possible to roll the fingers in the usual manner. If the fingers are not joined all the way to the tip it may be possible to get a "rolled" print by using finger blocks cut from a fingerprint card and fold them around the webbed digits to print the entire pattern. If the fingers are fully joined they will have separate patterning and, even if not susceptible to being rolled, can be printed effectively and classified properly so long as the digits are in order on the card even though it may not be possible to print the digits in their appropriate blocks.

More common than supernumerary digits or webbing are instances where fingers are missing. This is commonly the result of amputation although it may be congenital. The procedure is, very simply, to leave the finger block blank and indicate that the space is blank due to an amputated or missing finger. It is also very helpful to indicate approximately when the digit was lost because if it was amputated prior to the time the individual could have been printed for employment or as a result of being arrested, then it can save the person who will do the classification and searching of the fingerprints a substantial amount of work. If any part of the terminal phalange is still present it should be printed since it may possess some vestige of the pattern, making classification of the fingerprints easier. At times an amputation can be such that it is difficult to determine which digit has been removed. Unless the metacarpal bone for the finger has been removed completely, however, it is still usually possible to examine the hand and determine the digit that is missing.

It may be occasionally necessary to print a subject who would be

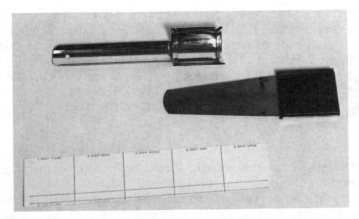

Figure 2.12 A post-mortem fingerprint kit with a "spoon," small ink pad, and strips cut from a fingerprint card.

subjected to great pain if printed in the normal manner because of injury or disease. Some individuals suffer from conditions which cause the fingers to curl toward the palm, making the securing of prints from the fingers or palms a difficult task. While it does seem unlikely that someone so afflicted would be likely to leave prints or impressions at a crime scene, it is possible. It is more likely, however, that the printing will be necessitated by a matter concerning personal identification requiring only fingerprints. It will be necessary at times, however, also to secure palm prints of such individuals.

If possible in such situations, it is preferrable to have the subject seated at a table or counter so that the arms and hands can be placed in a comfortable, relaxed position. The method of printing that is most successful is to ink the fingers with the roller, an ink paddle from a post-mortem kit (Figure 2.12), or the inked film previously described. The fingers are then printed on strips or blocks cut from a regular fingerprint card. This is accomplished by either using the curved "spoon" from the post-mortem kit or by manually curling the strip or block and carefully wrapping it around the finger. Care must be taken to prevent smearing the print. It may be necessary to make a number of prints of each finger in order to obtain a usable one, but perseverance should result in a set of prints that, except for the strips or blocks, is indistinguishable from a normally made set.

Printing the palms in these cases may be somewhat more difficult. If it is not possible to hold the hand flat for printing it will be necessary to print the palm area by area. If the palm is curled and creased, small areas can be flattened by stretching the skin. The area is then

inked and printed on small pieces of paper or card. It is usually possible, by this method, to print most or all of the palm. The individual
prints should be identified as to the area each represents so that they
can be (figuratively) put together to represent a complete palm print.
In those cases where it is just not possible to print part of the palm,
it is certainly very unlikely that the individual could have left a print
or impression of that part of the palm at a crime scene.

Printing the Deceased

Fortunately there is usually little difference between printing the deceased and the living with respect to either purpose or technique. For
the most part, the purpose of printing the deceased is to establish or
confirm identity. This is usually accomplished with an ordinary set
of fingerprints. If the deceased has a criminal record or has had an
occupation that required fingerprinting then identity can usually be
confirmed quite easily. If there is no possibility of such a record because of the youthfulness of the deceased or if the identity and history of the deceased is truly in doubt then it may also be necessary
to prepare palm prints. In some instances identity can be confirmed
by comparing such post-mortem prints with latent prints developed
on items known to have been handled by the person whom the deceased is suspected to be. It is also useful in some criminal cases to
be able to prove that the deceased was at a particular place or handled
a certain object—a gun, for instance. In this case finger and palm
prints would certainly be useful. The extent of the printing that is
done is often a matter of judgment but, because the deceased may not
be available for additional printing if it is found to be necessary at a
later date, it is preferable to prepare prints as extensive as *may* become necessary than to have to do without.

Generally, the techniques that are used for taking prints of the living suffice for printing the deceased. Provided the body is in relatively
good condition the primary difficulty is in overcoming the effects of
rigor. This can be overcome in a number of ways, the most drastic of
which is to sever the fingers (Figure 2.13) or even the entire hand.
Severing the fingers or the hand is usually necessary in only the most
extreme cases where the condition of the skin is such that ordinary
printing techniques cannot be used.

If the hands are in reasonably good condition, obtaining good prints
is usually accomplished by straightening the digits and flattening the
palm. It is often possible to "break" the rigor by forceably straightening the digits, which can then be printed using blocks or strips as
described for printing living individuals. If the fingers only are of concern, it is possible, and very simple, to print them by pressing on the

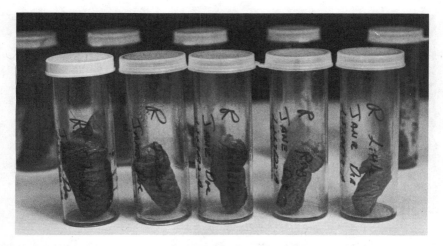

Figure 2.13 Severed fingers, separately packaged and marked.

finger just above the knuckle (Figure 2.14). This will straighten the finger and separate it from the others, making it easy to print. The palm can also be made similarly available for printing by bending it forward at the wrist. Although it may not be possible to print the palm as a whole by this technique, it is usually possible to get adequate prints by printing the various areas of the palm separately.

If breaking rigor is difficult or ineffective, or if the hand is so curled that the fingers or palm will not straighten sufficiently when pressed inward, it may be necessary to cut the tendons which cause the curling to occur. Such cutting is done at the joints of the base of the fingers and at the wrist. When straightened after cutting, the tendons will no longer resist and prevent the hand opening. In some places there are legal restrictions as to who may do such cutting of the deceased, so the printer should be certain that only legally designated persons perform this activity.

The primary difficult encountered in printing the deceased is the deep wrinkling or creasing of fingers and palms. This can often be overcome by stretching the affected skin. If the skin is still flexible, grasping the skin on the back of the finger and pinching will often remove most or all of the wrinkles. Wrinkles in the palm can usually be overcome by bending the fingers backward, if the tendons have not been cut. Alternatively, small areas of the palm can be flattened by stretching the skin with one hand while the other hand is used to ink and print. If this is not effective because the wrinkles are too deep or because the skin has begun to lose its flexibility, it will often be use-

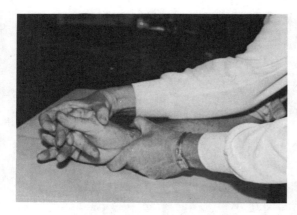

Figure 2.14 Straightening a finger for post-mortem printing.

ful to inject "tissue builder" into the finger or palm. This will cause the digit or an area of the palm to balloon or expand, removing the wrinkles and allowing good prints to be made.

It is possible to use ordinary water to expand the tissue and stretch the skin; however, subsequent printing pressures usually force the water back out of the hole caused by the syringe. For this reason, more viscous materials are usually used. Commercially available tissue builders may be simply highly viscous fluids or they may actually harden after injection. As a practical matter, if a commercial or "special preparation" is not available, almost any injectable substance can be used to advantage. The tissue builder should be injected in small amounts from a number of points around the periphery of the area of interest (Figure 2.15). Care should be taken to inject only as much as is needed to remove the wrinkles. If too much is injected, the skin may actually be damaged.

The condition of the skin can vary widely depending upon the circumstances of the death and the environmental and time factors involved before discovery. The hands, as well as the rest of the body, may mummify and become very dry, hard, and shrunken. At times the body may begin to liquify and the liquified fats *(adipocere)* will exude from the skin. The epidermis may become separated from the dermis; the entire skin, dermis and epidermis, may become separated from the underlying tissues (Figure 2.16). In any of these circumstances, successful printing is often a matter of imagination and caution. The printer's task is to obtain prints; whatever technique works is the appropriate one. Caution needs to be exercised since degradation of the quality of the skin by an unsuccessful technique may make further attempts futile.

If the condition of the skin is such that prints cannot be made by

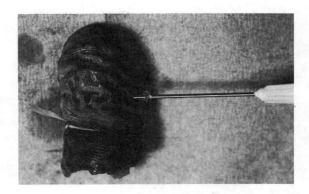

Figure 2.15 Injecting tissue builder.

ordinary techniques, or if such prints are not of adequate quality, then it is usually necessary to sever the fingers or hand. Severed fingers should be placed in individual jars and properly labeled (see Figure 2.13). It is, of course, not necessary to lable an entire hand as being left of right. Mummified or dried members may not need to placed in preservative immediately if at all, but unless the work is to commence at once, severed members in any other condition should be placed in a preservative such as formalin. Separated skin must be placed in an appropriate preservative and, because it may shrink and curl drastically, should be kept moist during all processing. Appropriate preservative solutions have an additional advantage in that they tend to toughen the skin, lessening the chance of damage with the necessary subsequent handling.

If the skin is sufficiently tough it may be possible to use tissue builder, if necessary, on the member and ink and print it normally. Good prints can also be obtained by removing the bone and most, but not all, of the internal tissue, securing it around one's own gloved finger or palm, and then printing normally (Figure 2.17). This particular technique requires an amount of practice that makes it impractical for most workers. Fortunately it is seldom necessary to have to resort to removing the skin to obtain good prints.

Occasionally the skin will be quite fragile and subject to damage if handled. Formaldehyde or formalin may help in this regard but, if additional toughening is required, a 5% solution of tannic acid may be useful. It may take 10–14 days for the skin to become strong enough to manipulate. Care should be exercised that complete fingers or hands do not become so toughened that the skin will not flatten enough for printing.

Perhaps the most useful tool for obtaining a record of friction ridges is a camera. If the skin is not too deeply wrinkled or if it can be

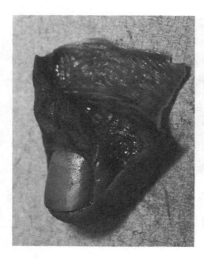

Figure 2.16 Skin sloughed from a finger after immersion in water for several days.

expanded with tissue builder, it is usually possible to photograph even the poorest quality skin. The drawback to photographs, however, is that the depth-of-field at the close focusing distances involved may necessitate a series of photographs in order fully to record the ridges as they go around the finger or edge of the palm. Sufficient contrast between the ridges and furrows can be achieved in some cases by dusting the ridges with fingerprint powder of an appropriate color and adjusting the light to produce the best rendition of the ridges. This may at times produce a photograph of light-colored ridges and dark furrows, but the tonality can be reversed photographically if necessary. Oblique lighting, while useful, depends upon shadows to create the necessary contrast; where the direction of the ridges paral-

Figure 2.17 A set of fingerprints from a cadaver immersed in water for several days.

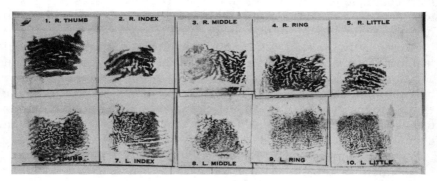

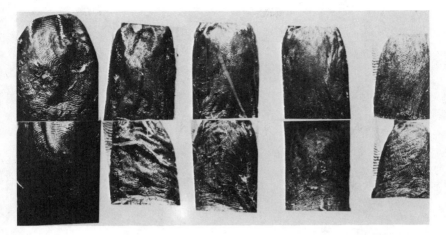

Figure 2.18 A set of "fingerprints" prepared with photographs of the fingers.

lels the direction of the light the detail will be faint or nonexistent.

When the skin has been removed from the hand by natural process or by the printer, if normal inking and printing is inadvisable or has been unsuccessful, it is usually simple to photograph. If the skin is thin and translucent, it can be placed between glass slides and photographed with transmitted light. The difference in thickness between the ridges and the valleys of the skin will allow different amounts of light to pass through and will cause quite sufficient contrast for comparison. Care must be taken that the skin does not dry during this operation because it will shrink and become useless.

If the intact fingers or palm are covered with adipocere and are slick and shiny, photography is also a possibility. Proper adjustment of the angle of the lighting can allow photographs to be made relying on the difference in reflection between the slick tops of the ridges and the shadowed furrows. In one instance the author did not even remove the fingers from the vials in which they were received. They were easily photographed through the clear plastic of the vials (Figure 2.18).

Other techniques may be utilized at the judgment or whim of the printer. It is sometimes useful to dust the ridges with latent print powder and make a lift with lifting tape. It is also possible to make plaster molds of the fingers and palms which can be cast with flexible casting material again and again until a good print is obtained. There is such a broad range of conditions that may occur that it is not possible to define a particular technique as being always appropriate for a given set of circumstances.

Classification

3

The classification of prints of fingers, palms, and soles is very simply the process of putting them into groupings, the members of which all have some recognizable overall similarity. The primary usefulness of such classification is to allow the prints to be filed in a manner that will allow the examiner to search a print of unknown or questionable origin through the file without having to compare it to every record print on file. With a properly ordered file of record prints, the examiner need compare the unknown or questioned print only with other prints that have the same class characteristics.

The most common type of file is that based on a classification derived from the class characteristics of all of the 10 fingers of individuals. In this type of system the classification is a descriptive file number that enables the filing of each fingerprint card with other fingerprint cards which have the same class characteristics in the same fingers. A number of such classification systems have been developed for the purpose, allowing the orderly filing of record prints. The most commonly used of these are the *Henry* and the *Vucetich* systems. It is doubtful, however, that either of these gentlemen would recognize the systems that bear their names because it has been necessary over the decades to modify and expand those systems to allow them to accomodate files of a size that were not forseeable when they were devised.

The use of classification systems based on the class characteristics of all 10 fingers is generally limited to determining the identity of an individual who is availabe to provide fingerprints. Because of this, systems been developed which allow the filing of single-hand (five-finger) cards and of single fingerprints. Although these systems generally utilize additional class characteristics of the individual fingers, they are still limited to relatively small files simply because 10 fingers can provide more classifiable data than can one or five fingers. The purpose of these types of file is to allow searching of prints found at the scenes of crimes in an attempt to determine the identity of the responsible party.

Classification schemes designed for the orderly filing of palm and sole prints exist primarily for the same reason as the classification systems for single fingerprints—the identification of those responsible for crimes. It is seldom necessary to have to resort to palm or sole prints to identify persons who are available to be printed. Such classifications are useful and, like those for fingerprints, are based on class characteristics. Unlike fingerprints, the class characteristics of palm and sole prints are determined by the appearance of defined areas within the print, not on the appearance of the entire print.

Instruction in the classification systems devised by Henry and Vucetich, and to an extent that of Battley, are beyond the scope of this book. Knowledge of classifying individual prints is important for those interested in the forensic application of the comparison and identification of friction skin for two very basic reasons. The first reason is that the person who works in this field, just as any other forensic scientist, needs to be able to communicate with others in the same field. Just as the firearms examiner should know and be able to articulate the difference between a revolver and a pistol, the fingerprint examiner should know and be able to articulate the difference between an arch and a whorl.

The second reason is that a thorough understanding of the class characteristics of prints can make the task of comparing two prints and determining whether or not they were made by the same individual easier. This understanding will also make the examiner better able to explain the rationale used to arrive at the determination of identity or nonidentity between two prints.

Fingerprints

Classifications systems rely on a limited number of descriptors. Each defined class of fingerprint pattern, commonly called a pattern type, contains patterns that can vary considerably in general appearance. To the extent that it has been convenient, the larger classes of prints are further divided into subclasses. While each class and subclass of pattern can be, and is, specifically defined for the system used, there is a continuum or flow from one pattern type to another that defies absolute delineation between types. That is, there are points in any classification system where it will be impossible to determine if a particular print is of one pattern type or another.

The continuum of pattern types progresses from the simplest pattern, the arch, to the most complex whorl subtype. The following sections discuss and describe these pattern types. The descriptions and terminology used will be that of the Henry classification system that is currently used in the United States. The reader who works in an area where another system is in use will still find this valuable, however; all classification systems are based on the same fingerprint patterns although the definitions and terminology may vary slightly.

Also, the differences between pattern types is not nearly so clearcut as that between revolvers and pistols. Because filing schemes began fairly simply and on a small scale, the rules and definitions were fairly broad. As the files grew, greater definition was necessary and the rules for classification grew more complex. These changes did not emanate from a single source and so, unfortunately, there are many variations in the interpretation of pattern types and subtypes even among those who, for instance, use the *Henry* system. These variations occur primarily where one pattern approaches the appearance of another. Therefore a technician trained at one agency might consider a pattern to be clearly of one type while another technician trained in a different place would consider it to be unequivocally another pattern type. This is not necessarily a disabling situation so long as each is aware of the potential difference in interpretation and can articulate their own rules and definitions.

. The rules and definitions used by the author are those he learned while working at the FBI Identification Division and they have served well. However, an awareness of the differences that do or may exist has facilitated communication and prevented, surely, many disputes.

The Plain Arch

The plain arch pattern is the simplest and, perhaps, the least distinctive pattern. Very simply, in this pattern the ridges flow from one side to the other with no (1) angles of 90° or less, (2) ridges that recurve and go out the same side from which they entered, or (3) upthrusting ridges that do not follow the general flow of the ridges. In Figure 3.1 it can be seen that, even as simple as the pattern is, there are some not-so-subtle differences that make them each individually describable. These differences do, in fact, constitute additional class characteristics beyond the general description of plain arch.

In print (a) it can be seen that the apex of each arching ridge falls very nearly on a straight, vertical line. In print (b), a line connecting the apices of the ridges slopes generally down and toward the left.

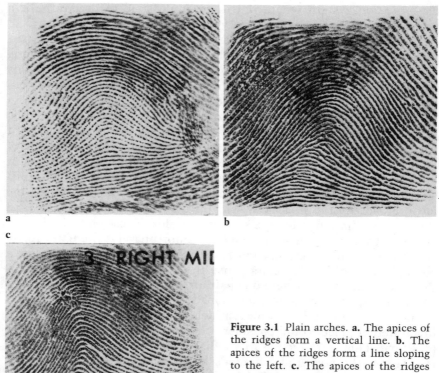

a

b

c

Figure 3.1 Plain arches. **a.** The apices of the ridges form a vertical line. **b.** The apices of the ridges form a line sloping to the left. **c.** The apices of the ridges arc, concavity to the left.

Print (**c**) differs in that the line described by the apices of the arching ridges describes an arc, the inside of which is to the left.

These are not, of course, all the possible variations in appearance of the plain arch pattern. Such variations can also be affected by external factors. A pattern such as (**a**) can be made to appear similar to (**b**) or even (**c**) if sufficient distortion is introduced when the print is made. Distortion can affect a print only so much, however, before it becomes apparent, or at least suspected. For instance, for the arc apparent in (**a**) to appear as an arc similar to that in (**b**) would probably require sufficient stretching or slipping of the skin that the print would be obviously smudged.

The Tented Arch

The tented arch pattern is, in its simplest form, only slightly more complex than the plain arch. Tented arches increase in complexity as they approach the appearance of the loop pattern. Before the tented arch can be fully comprehended, one must become familiar with terms that are most easily discussed as they apply to loop patterns; the reader may want to return to this section after reading the discussion of loop patterns.

In the tented arch the smooth flow of ridges from one side of the print to the other is interrupted either by a ridge forming an angle of 90° or less or by an upthrusting ridge that does not follow the general flow of the ridges. A third type of tented arch is one that meets only two of the three requirements of a loop: a recurving ridge, a ridge count across a recurving ridge, and a delta.

Figure 3.2a is an angular-type tented arch because the angle formed by the ridges at the center of the pattern is obviously less than 90°. Figure 3.2b may or may not be an angular-type tented arch because the ridge which is sharply bent may be interpreted to be sharply curved rather than angular. However, even if the formation is not angular the pattern would still be a tented arch because of the upthrusting ridges at the center. As can be easily surmised, if such a print is made with excessive pressure, or if distortion is introduced, or if the developing medium is used too liberally, the angularity can be obscured, causing it to seem rounded. The pattern could then appear to be a plain arch or perhaps an upthrust-type tented arch.

Figures 3.3a and 3.3b are tented arches because they have one or more ridges that rise in the center of the pattern that do not follow the smooth flow of the ridges from one side of the pattern to the other. This *upthrust* need not be vertical nor even very long, provided it does not follow the flow of the ridges above and below it. For a

Figure 3.2 a. Angular-type tented arch. **b.** Upthrust-type tented arch. The ridge over the upthrusting ridges *may* form an angle.

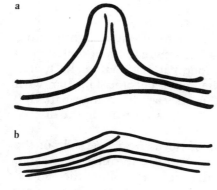

Figure 3.3 **a.** Upthrust-type tented arch. **b.** Upthrust-type tented arch. The upthrusting ridge does not follow the flow of the ridges on either side.

feature to qualify as an upthrust it must be longer than it is wide: a dot on top of another ridge does not qualify as an upthrust. Any ridge that does not follow the flow of the ridges above and below it is an upthrust. Even a ridge that is essentially flat is an upthrust if it does not turn down when the ridges above and below it do, as in Figure 3.3b.

Figures 3.4a, b, c demonstrate tented arch patterns that approach being loop patterns because they possess two of the three requirements of the loop. The distinction between these patterns and a loop pattern is that each lacks a recurve, ridge count, or a delta (see next section). Figure 3.4a would be a good loop pattern except that the only possible placement of the delta is on the recurve which prevents having a ridge count across a recurving ridge. Figure 3.4b shows a pattern that has a good delta and even a ridge count, but it does not have a recurve. Figure 3.4c shows a print that seems to have all three re-

Figure 3.4 **a.** A tented arch that would be a loop but for the absence of a delta. **b.** A tented arch that would be a loop but for the absence of a recurve. **c.** A tented arch that would be a loop but for the ridge abutting the recurve between the shoulders.

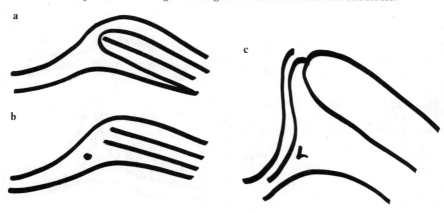

quirements of a loop. What prevents this pattern from being a loop is the ridge abutting the recurve and not passing in front of the delta. The abutment, by spoiling the recurve, leaves only a delta and a ridge count which are but two of the requirements of a loop.

As with other patterns, this pattern can appear to be another pattern if it is inaccurately recorded. The loop-type tented arch may, at times, appear to be an upthrust-type tented arch, or it may appear to be a loop pattern. Also if each of the subtypes of tented arches is considered a distinct class by itself, it is apparent that each can have other describable class characteristics just as does the plain arch. These include such things as the degree of angularity, the slope, length, and number of upthrusting ridges, and the side from which the upthrusting or recurving ridges enter. Even the distance between the key features and the crease between the joint of the finger can be considered to be class characteristics.

Figure 3.5 shows a number of examples of tented arch patterns. Patterns (a) and (b) are unequivocally tented arches. Pattern (c), here appearing to be a tented arch because of the distinct, though very short, upthrust could very easily appear to be a plain arch if printed with too much ink or pressure. Patterns **d** and **e** are tented arches of the loop type that, if printed differently, could easily be interpreted as good loop patterns. Because of this, all loop-type tented arches are referenced to loop patterns as a matter of course. This means that for classification and file searching purposes they are considered in both possible interpretations.

The Loop

To be able to classify the loop (and the loop-type tented arch) accurately, it is necessary to learn to distinguish certain features in accordance with some rather finely drawn definitions. To be a loop a pattern must have (1) one (and only one) delta, (2) a ridge that goes out or tends to go out the same side from which it entered, and (3) at least one ridge that crosses a line drawn between the core and the delta. The key features or points to be located are thus the delta and the core.

The *delta* is defined as the point on a ridge (not the ridge itself) that is nearest to, and in front of, the divergence of the type lines. To locate that point it is, of course, necessary to find the type lines and the point at which they diverge. The *type lines* are the two innermost ridges that start parallel, diverge (or tend to diverge), and surround (or tend to surround) the pattern area (Figure 3.6). It is simple to locate the approximate area in which the delta is located because it is a roughly triangular area in which the ridges radiate outward in three directions.

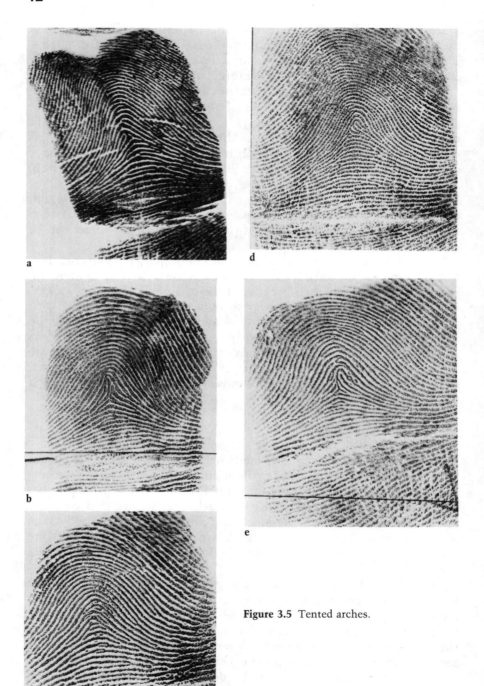

Figure 3.5 Tented arches.

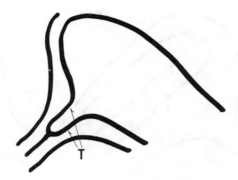

Figure 3.6 Type lines (T).

Other rules have been devised in order to make determination of the delta consistent and accurate.

1. The delta may not be placed on a bifurcation that does not open toward the core.
2. If more than one bifurcation would otherwise qualify as the location of the delta, the delta must be placed at the bifurcation that is nearest to the core (Figure 3.7a).
3. The delta may not be placed in the middle of a ridge that runs between the type lines, but must be placed on the end nearer the core (Figure 3.7b).
4. If a bifurcation and another ridge would be equally qualified for placement of the delta, the bifurcation is chosen (Figure 3.7c).

Figure 3.7 a. If the delta (D) could be placed on more than one bifurcation, the one nearer the core is selected. **b.** If the delta is placed on a ridge that runs between the type lines, it is placed on the end nearer the core. **c.** The bifurcation is selected for the placement of the delta when a bifurcation and another feature are equally qualified.

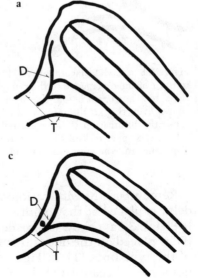

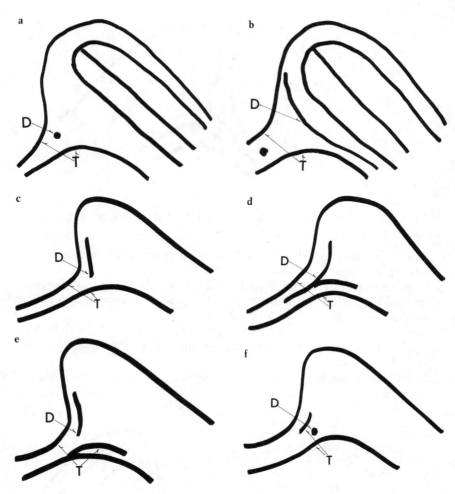

Figure 3.8 a. Delta placement. **b.** The delta is not placed on the dot because it is not in front of the divergence of the type lines. **c.** The delta is placed as shown because the ridge does not begin before the divergence of the type lines. **d.** The delta is placed as shown even though the bifurcated ridge would also qualify as the upper type line because the bifurcation is the preferred delta. **e.** The type lines are the two *innermost* ridges, the upper fork of the bifurcation is therefore selected as the lower type line. **f.** Type lines may be very short provided they start parallel.

Remember, the bifurcation or other feature is not the delta, but the delta is placed at that point.

Figure 3.8a–f shows some delta placements. In Figure 3.8a the delta (D) is placed on the dot as it is the first ridge in front of the divergence of the type lines (T). In Figure 3.8b the delta is placed on the continuous ridge because the dot is not in front of the divergence of the

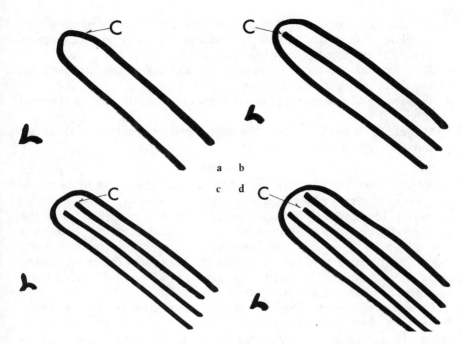

Figure 3.9 a. Core (C) placement for a single recurve with no abutments or inclusions. **b.** Core placement for a recurve with a single rod. **c.** Core placement for a recurve with two rods. **d.** Core placement for a recurve with an odd number of rods.

type lines. In Figure 3.8c the delta is placed on the end of the ridge nearer the divergence of the type lines because, unlike Figure 3.7b, the ridge does not go between the type lines.

The delta in Figure 3.8d is placed at the point of bifurcation, even though the bifurcating ridge does start parallel with both indicated type lines. This is so because the bifurcation is always to be preferred as a delta unless another feature is clearly nearer the divergence of the type lines. In Figure 3.8e the type lines are selected as being the *innermost* ridges that start parallel and diverge, and the delta is therefore placed at *D*. In Figure 3.8f the upper type line is placed at the short ridge and the delta is therefore at the dot. Type lines need not be very long, provided they start parallel and diverge (or *tend* to diverge) and surround the pattern area.

The *core*, like the delta, can be roughly located by the appearance of the pattern, the core being near where the innermost recurve begins turning to go back out the way it came in.

1. In the pattern with a clean, smooth recurve, with no ridges inside the recurving ridge, the core is placed at the point where the innermost recurve begins to turn back upon itself (Figure 3.9a).

2. If there is a single ridge (or *rod*) within that recurve that rises to or above the point where the recurve begins, then the core is placed at the top of that ridge (Figure 3.9b).
3. If two ridges rise above that point, the top of the one farthest from the delta is selected as the core (Figure 3.9c).
4. If there is an odd number of such rods, the center one is selected (Figure 3.9d).
5. If there is an even number, the center pair is treated as if there are but two rods within the recurve.

The core may only be placed on or within a *recurving* ridge (not an angular formation) that is (1) free of ridges that abut it at 90° between the points of recurve and (2) free of appendages between the points of recurve (the shoulders) that do not pass in front of the delta. If the only recurving ridge is spoiled by such an abutment, the pattern is not a loop but is a loop-type tented arch. If the only recurve has a ridge flowing smoothly from between the shoulders that touches the delta, or goes outside the delta, the pattern is a loop and is not a loop-type tented arch (see Figure 3.4c).

To be considered a "good" recurve, a ridge must be free of appendages that abut it at right angles between the shoulders of the recurve. Figure 3.10a shows a recurve spoiled by such an abutment. Since the abutting ridge also recurves and passes in front of the delta, it qualifies as a good or sufficient recurve and the core is placed as shown. Figure 3.10b also shows a pattern with an appendage on a good recurve but, because the appendage does not abut the recurve at a 90° angle, it does not spoil the recurve and the core is placed as shown.

Figure 3.10 a. Core placement for a recurve spoiled by an abutting ridge that also recurves. **b.** The core is placed on the innermost recurving ridge. The appended ridge does not join at right angles.

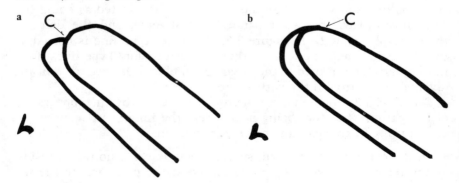

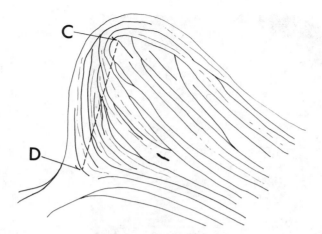

Figure 3.11 Ridge counting. There are ten ridge counts between the delta and the core. The bifurcation at the second ridge count from the delta recieves two ridge counts because the line crossed the point of bifurcation. The delta and core are not counted. Incipient ridges are not counted but dots are counted if as thick and broad as the ridges on either side.

The reason for these rather finely drawn rules for placing the delta and core of the loop pattern is that it is necessary in order to ensure that ridge counting is accurate from classifier to classifier. *Ridge counting* is a method for determining an additional class characteristic of the loop pattern: the number of ridges that touch or cross an imaginary line between the delta and the core. The ridges upon which the delta and core are placed are not counted, but ridges connected to those are counted. Both sides of an island are counted and, if the line crosses the point at which a ridge bifurcates, both forks of the bifurcation are counted. Incipient ridges are not counted, although dots are counted if they are as thick and broad as the ridges on either side. Ridge counting is illustrated in Figure 3.11.

Ridge counting and all other classification and comparison tasks are usually accomplished using a magnifier. Commonly these devices magnify the print to 4–5 times actual size (Figure 3.12). To count ridges accurately a reticle (Figure 3.13) is placed in the base of the magnifier. The reticle has a line across it which is placed so that it crosses the delta and the core as precisely as possible. Other types of reticle are available for other classification systems. Figure 3.13b shows a Battley disk for use in classifying prints according to the Battley single print system. In this system the ridges are not counted; instead, the distance between the delta and core is determined by placing the central dot at the apex of the innermost recurving ridge and determining in which ring the delta appears.

Figure 3.12 A fingerprint through a magnifier.

In addition to the classification of loop and the number of ridges intervening between the delta and core, these patterns are also categorized according to the slope of the ridges. In working with single prints where the hand, left or right, that made the print is unknown, or when working in a file designed for searching single prints, the

Figure 3.13 a. A "Henry" disk (reticle). **b.** A "Battley" disk (reticle).

a   b

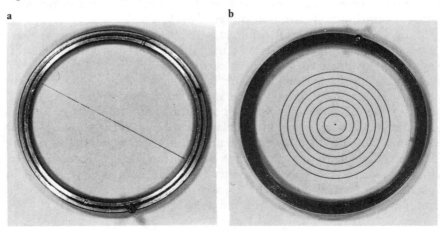

usual designation is either left or right slope. The *slope* is determined by tracing the ridges from the core down and to the side of the print. If the trace is down and to the left, it is a *left-slope loop;* if down and to the right, it is a *right-slope loop.*

If the classification of the print is determined for use in a file designed for searching full sets of fingerprints, the terms generally used are ulnar and radial. These terms relate to the position of the ulna and radial bones of the forearm. If the slope of the print is toward the ulna, the outside bone of the arm, the pattern is termed an *ulnar loop.* If the slope is toward the radial, the inside bone of the arm, then the pattern is a *radial loop.* Thus, for the right hand, an ulnar loop is right slope and a radial loop is left slope; the opposite is true in the left hand.

The term *loop,* as with the other patterns discussed, is merely a general designation for prints possessing certain features. Within this general classification the appearance of the patterns can differ quite remarkably. Loop patterns can be very small having but one recurving ridge. Some loop patterns can have many ridges between the delta and the core, although ridge counts greater than 30 are quite unusual. The looping ridges may be straight or curved, vertical or horizontal. The recurve may be very tight and narrow or it may appear very broad and gently curved. All of these characteristics can be considered class characteristics and can, of course, vary somewhat between two prints of the same finger due to the method of recording. Some of the various appearances of the loop pattern are illustrated in Figure 3.14.

The Whorl

The pattern designation of *whorl* includes the most complexly shaped of the fingerprint patterns. Put most succinctly, a whorl is any pattern that possesses two or more deltas with a recurve in front of each that is unspoiled by an abutting ridge or an appendage connecting it to the delta; alternatively, it is any pattern that does not conform to the definition of any other pattern. Whereas the loop has two defined subclasses, the whorl has four: the plain whorl, the central-pocket whorl, the double-loop whorl, and the accidental whorl.

All whorls can be further subdivided and described as having a meet, an inner, or an outer tracing. This is accomplished by tracing the ridges from the left delta toward the right delta. If the traced ridge meets the right delta or comes within three ridges from it at its closest point, the pattern has a *meet* tracing. If there are three or more ridges intervening between the traced ridge and the right delta, then the pattern has either an *inner* or an *outer* tracing, depending on whether the tracing is toward the inside of the delta or the outside. Figures 3.15a–c, shows examples of inner, meeting, and outer tracing.

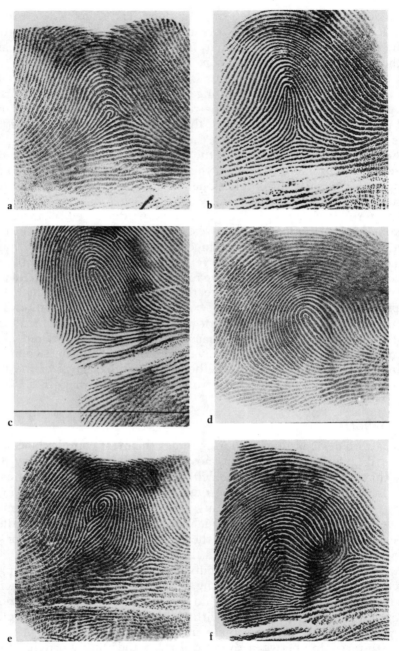

Figure 3.14 Loop patterns. **a.** Left slope, 2 counts. **b.** Left slope, 4 counts. **c.** Right slope, 12 counts. **d.** Right slope, 23 counts. **e.** Left slope, 17 counts. **f.** Left slope nutant (nodding), 7 counts.

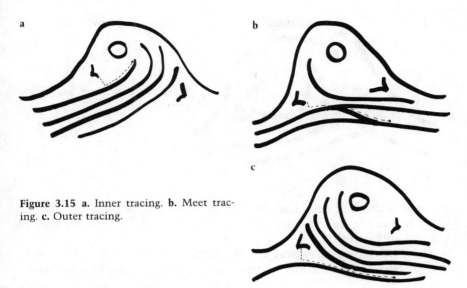

Figure 3.15 a. Inner tracing. **b.** Meet tracing. **c.** Outer tracing.

The *plain whorl* is the simplest of the whorl subtypes. It is a pattern with two deltas with at least one ridge that forms a complete circuit that passes in front of both deltas. A line between the deltas must touch or cross at least one of the ridges forming the circuit. A ridge that abuts the circuit forming ridge on the side toward one of the deltas spoils that ridge for consideration as a recurving ridge *for that delta*. The ridge forming the circuit may be circular, spiral, oval, or any other shape as long as it is possible to trace it from top to bottom and back to the top. The ridge forming the complete circuit need not be a single ridge, but may be made up of a ridge that is broken or a number of short ridges that, taken together, form a complete circuit. Figure 3.16 shows the minimum requirements of a whorl pattern: two deltas with a recurve in front of each. The recurves need not be connected as they are here. Figure 3.17 shows the minimum requirements of a *plain* whorl: two deltas with at least one

Figure 3.16 Minimum requirements of a whorl.

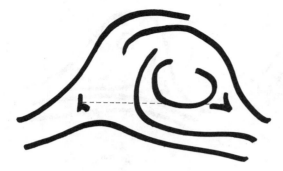

Figure 3.17 Determining a plain whorl.

recurve in front of each and the line between the deltas touching one ridge inside the delta nearer the core. Figure 3.18 shows a number of plain whorl patterns.

The *central-pocket* whorl is very similar to the plain whorl with the exception that the line drawn between the deltas does not cross

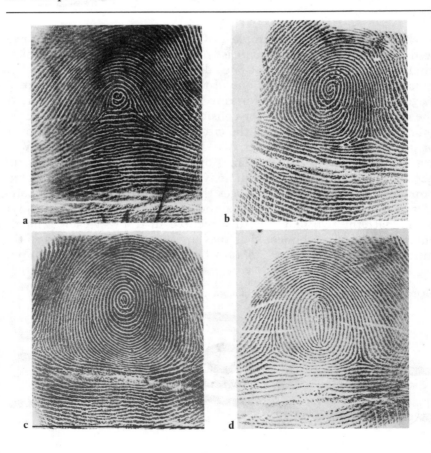

or touch a ridge that is inside the type lines of the delta nearer the core (Figure 3.19). Thus, generally speaking, one delta appears to be substantially closer to the center of the pattern than the other. In all cases this should be checked, however, since the flow of the ridges and the placement of the deltas on the perimeter of recurving ridges can cause a print that seems to be apparently a member of one subtype to be technically of the other. There is one special case situation within the central-pocket whorl subtype: the *obstruction-type* central-pocket whorl. In this pattern the line of flow of a loop pattern is crossed at right angles by a straight ridge. The line of flow of a pattern is determined by drawing a line between the inner delta and the apex of the recurving ridge. If a straight ridge crosses this line of flow at right angles, the pattern is considered to be a central-pocket whorl. There need be no recurring ridge (Figure 3.20).

The *double-loop* whorl is somewhat more complex than the plain or central-pocket whorl in that it is a combination of two distinct loop patterns. In some systems a distinction is made that divides this

e

f

Figure 3.18 Plain whorl patterns. **a.** Meet tracing. **b.** Inner tracing. **c.** Outer tracing. **d.** Inner tracing. **e.** Inner tracing. **f.** Outer tracing.

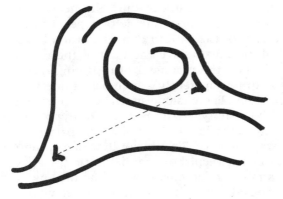

Figure 3.19 Determining a central-pocket whorl.

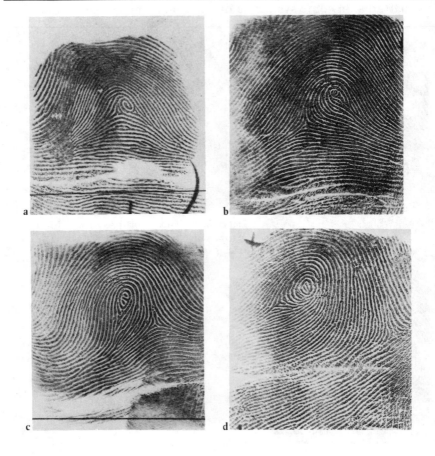

subtype into two more subtypes: the *twinned-loop* and the *lateral-pocket loop* whorls. In the twinned-loop whorl, the ridges traced from the cores of each loop exit the pattern on opposite sides. In the lateral-pocket loop whorl, the ridges traced from the separate cores exit on the same side of the pattern. In the Henry classification system, however, no such distinction is made.

The double-loop whorl has two deltas and two separate and distinct loops. This means that there must be two recurving ridges that are unspoiled by abutments between the shoulders of the recurves, or points where the recurving begins and ends; also, the recurves must not be connectd to a delta by an appendage, nor be intertwined with each other (Figure 3.21a). If it is possible to trace a continuous ridge from one of the cores to the other, then the pattern may still be a double-loop whorl (Figure 3.21b), if the connection does not consti-

Figure 3.20 Central-pocket whorl patterns. **a.** Meet tracing. **b.** Outer tracing. **c.** Inner tracing. **d.** Inner tracing. **e.** Outer tracing. **f.** Inner tracing.

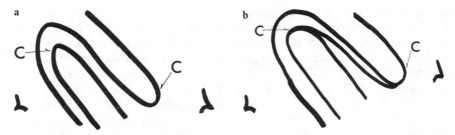

Figure 3.21 a. The basic requirements of the double-loop whorl. **b.** The two recurves of the double-loop whorl may be connected as long as they are formed by separate ridges and neither is spoiled by an abutting ridge.

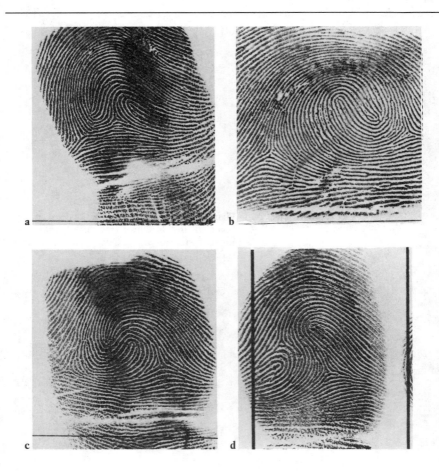

tute an appendage connecting the shoulders of the two loops. Figure 3.22 shows a number of double-loop whorls.

The *accidental whorl* is a pattern having three or more deltas, or having all the characteristics of two or more different pattern types (excluding the plain arch); it is a pattern that does not conform to the definition of any previously defined pattern. Thus the accidental whorl may appear as an otherwise ordinary whorl pattern that has three deltas, or it may be a combination of a loop and a whorl (Figure 3.23a), a loop and a tented arch (Figure 3.23b), or a highly unusual pattern that defies definition (Figure 3.24). Figure 3.25 illustrates a number of variants of the accidental whorl pattern.

Whorls generally have a definite slope that is easily determined by the line of flow. The exception to this is the very symmetrical pattern in which both deltas are equidistant from the core area of the pattern.

e

f

Figure 3.22 Double-loop whorl patterns. **a.** Outer tracing, lateral pocket. **b.** Outer tracing, lateral pocket. **c.** Meet tracing, lateral pocket. **d.** Inner tracing, *twinned loop.* **e.** Inner tracing, lateral pocket. **f.** Inner tracing, lateral pocket.

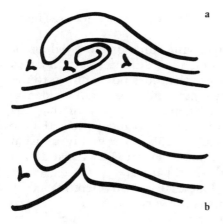

Figure 3.23 a. Accidental whorl; loop and whorl. **b.** Accidental whorl; loop and tented arch.

Whorls also, because they are the most complex of the various pattern types, can present an extremely broad range of appearance ranging from the simplest single circuiting ridge to combinations of a number of pattern types. Whorls can be symmetrical or asymmetrical, circular or spiral, round or oval, or any combination of these characteristics. Each characteristic and each combination can be considered to represent classes. There is, of course, the ever-present effect of distortion that may modify the appearance of a print to some degree that needs to be considered. However, as with any such print, if the distortion is substantial, it will usually be detectable.

Palm Prints

Palm print classification systems differ from those for fingerprints in that where fingerprints are conveniently small with the patterning confined to essentially one area, palm prints are quite large and have

Figure 3.24 An unusual pattern, this would be classified as an accidental whorl because it does not conform to the definitions for any other pattern types.

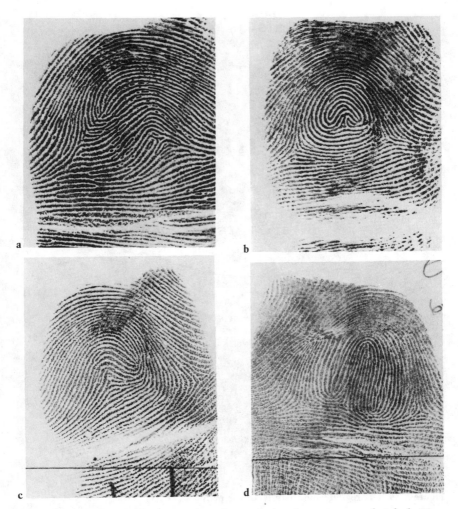

Figure 3.25 Accidental whorl patterns. **a.** Inner tracing, loop over tented arch. **b.** Meet tracing, three deltas. **c.** Inner tracing, loop over tented arch. **d.** Outer tracing, three deltas.

a number of areas of unrelated patterning. (The areas are unrelated for practical purposes, just as are fingerprints.) Classifying palm prints involves dividing the palm into a number of regions and then determining the presence or absence of triradii and patterns. The regions of the palm are shown in Figure 3.26.

The palm is easily divided into three primary regions: the interdigital, the thenar, and the hypothenar. The *interdigital* or palmar area is that area at the distal end of the palm, just below the fingers. The

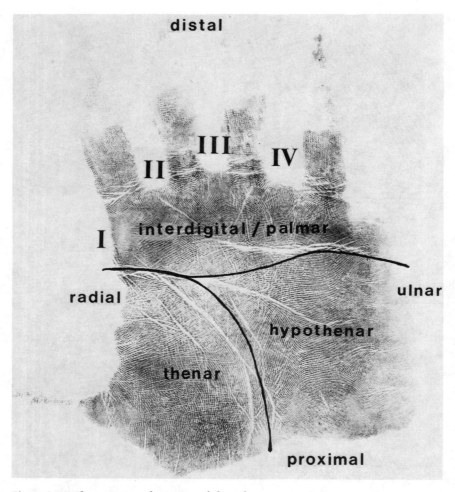

Figure 3.26 The regions and margins of the palm.

more complex systems divide this area into four parts. The first interdigital space is that between the thumb and index finger; the second is between the index and middle fingers; the third, between the middle and ring; and the fourth, between the ring and little fingers. Patterning in these areas, if any, usually consists of loop patterns with the ridges entering and leaving the palm between the fingers. Whorls do occasionally appear in this area. Because it is generally difficult to determine a boundary between the first interdigital space and the *thenar*, these are usually considered together, leaving the other three interdigital areas to be considered as a separate, distinct area. Sometimes referred to as the *palmar* region, this area is more easily susceptable to definition than is a region that encompasses all four interdigital spaces. The palmar area may be defined as the area bounded distally by the fingers and proximally by the distal transverse crease and the radial extension of the proximal transverse crease. These major creases of the palm are illustrated in Figure 3.27.

The thenar–first interdigital area is roughly bounded by the radial and distal margins of the palm and by the radial longitudinal crease and the upper or most radial portion of the proximal transverse crease. Patterning in this area is uncommon but does occur often enough to make it useful for classification. Such patterning usually consists of loop patterns, with an occasional whorl appearing. Loop patterns here generally enter from the proximal or radial direction and also from the first interdigital space. For classification purposes, the presence of a pattern is usually coded and its origin used for further subdivision.

The *hypothenar* is the area bounded by the distal and ulnar margins of the palm and by the radial longitudinal crease and the distal transverse crease. This area, like the others, is subject to patterning with loops, whorls, arches, and combinations of these. Classification systems usually take into account the type of pattern present and the margin or side from which it originates: distal, proximal, ulnar, or radial (Figure 3.27). Additionally, consideration is usually given to the position of the "delta," or *triradius*—the area or point from which ridges radiate in three directions—that is usually present near the proximal margin of the hypothenar.[1] This is usually considered with respect to its distance from the wrist or "bracelet" creases at the proximal margin of the palm.

Because the hypothenar is often devoid of specific patterning, the featureless plain arch configuration predominating, descriptors are often assigned to the delta itself in order to provide more groupings and, thus, fewer prints in each section of the file. These subgroups may be selected on the basis of how and whether the ridges meet at the delta formation. Ridges from three directions may meet at a single point, at three points (forming a triangle), or not at all. On the basis of these or other similar groupings it is possible to subdivide further an otherwise characterless field of ridges.

Palm prints commonly have five triradii: one below each finger and the "carpal delta," the triradius near the proximal margin of the palm, associated with the thumb. Additional triradii are almost always as-

---

[1]The term "delta" is only technically correct when the formation appears in conjunction with a pattern such as a loop or a whorl. Such a formation that is not associated with a pattern having recurving ridges cannot be a delta as defined for fingerprint classification because a delta is defined with respect to "typelines" which must surround a pattern. If there is no pattern, there is no delta.

62

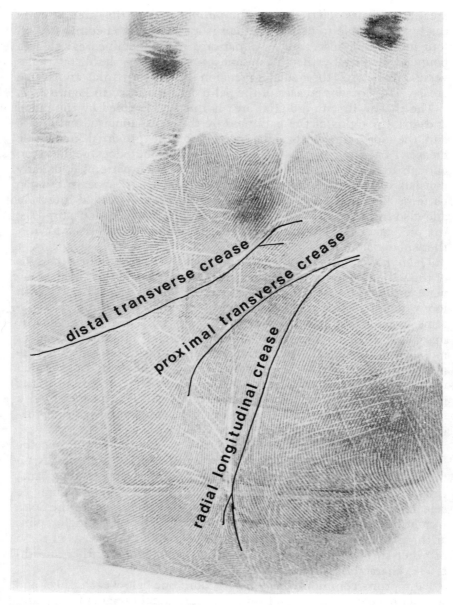

Figure 3.27 Major flexion creases of the palm.

sociated with the formation of recurves and are properly termed deltas. Each recurving formation implies one additional delta to accompany it; therefore, a palm print with one loop formation would have six triradial forms (five triradii and one delta). If a whorl is present there will be seven triradial forms, since a whorl has two recurves. When this does not appear to hold for a particular palm print—i.e., if there is patterning without concomitant triradial forms, or if there is an additional triradius without an associated recurring ridge formation—then it can be suspected that the palm was not fully printed, or that the friction skin does not continue far enough to allow the pattern to form completely.

A number of palm prints are illustrated in Figure 3-28a–g. Figure 3.28a shows a palm print that can be described as having a number of class characteristics. The thenar shows no patterning, being essentially an open field of smoothly flowing ridges. The hypothenar shows a radial loop pattern and the carpal delta is quite low. There are no patterns present in the palmar region, however, and there are only three triradii, there being no triradius below the ring finger.

The palm print in Figure 3.28b exhibits no patterning in either thenar or hypothenar and the carpal delta again is quite low (this is common). There are distal loops in the third and fourth interdigital spaces and an area of convergence approaching a loop pattern in the second interdigital area.

Figure 3.28c shows no patterning in the thenar but does have a whorl in the hypothenar and three deltas with the carpal delta being quite low. The third interdigital area shows a loop formation.

Figure 3.28d is a palm print with a tented arch pattern below the ring finger and an ulnar loop in the hypothenar, bracketed by a very low carpal delta and another delta that is quite high. The carpal delta is unprinted but its existence and location are indicated by the diverging ridges near the proximal margin of the palm. The distance between the core of the loop formation and each of the deltas can be used as additional class characteristics.

A very significant class characteristic appears in the palm print in Figure 3.28e: the pattern vestige in the hypothenar. Although it may at first seem to be an ulnar loop, there is actually no loop present; the ridges simply come to an end near the vertical ridges at the center of the palm.

In Figure 3.28f, the significant class characteristics are the vertical arch in the hypothenar and the lack of a triradius below the ring finger. The palm print in Figure 3.28g would have very common class characteristics except for the existence of the two whorl patterns in the thenar–first interdigital area. This is a very unusual occurrence.

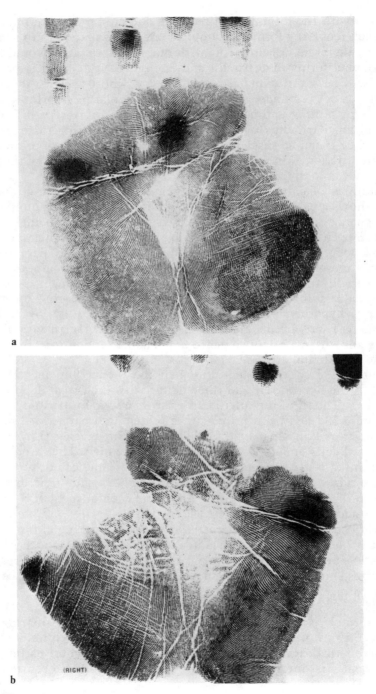

Figure 3.28 a.–g. Palm prints. See text for descriptions.

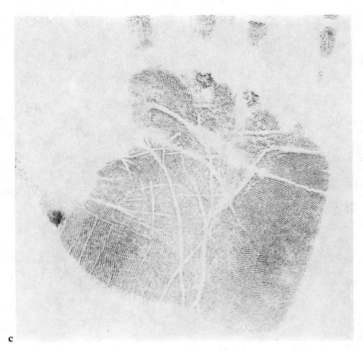

c

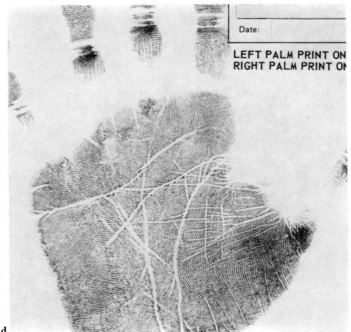

Date:

LEFT PALM PRINT ON
RIGHT PALM PRINT ON

d

(continued)

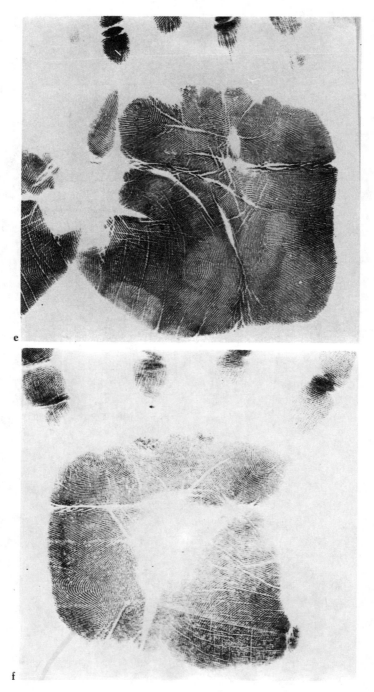

Figure 3.28 a.–g. Palm prints. See text for descriptions.

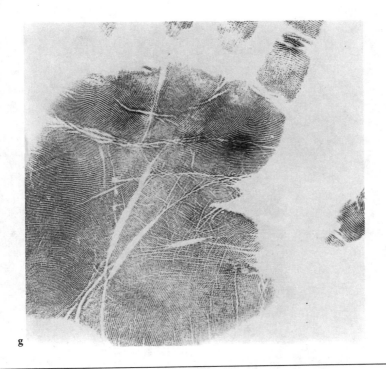

g

Sole Prints

The general designation of sole prints includes not only the prints of the sole of the foot, but also of the toes. Toes and soles have all of the same characteristics as fingers and palms and are subject to the same classification techniques. It is unusual for sole prints to be classified and filed, however, because the work involved in establishing and maintaining such a file is difficult to justify in light of the very occasional use it might receive. Also, the shape of the foot is, generally, such that evidence prints from scenes of crimes rarely possess any distinctive patterning except that from the ball of the foot; the other areas that possess patterning do not generally come into contact with the surface (Figure 3.29).

In very large file systems concerned with personal identification as a primary function, sole print files can have usefulness in maintaining the continuity of identity for individuals who have no hands. Such individuals might apply for jobs requiring positive identification, need their identities confirmed to establish eligibility for pension or other benefits, or engage in criminal activity. The Federal Bureau of Investigation therefore does maintain a file of sole prints even though it is used only occasionally.

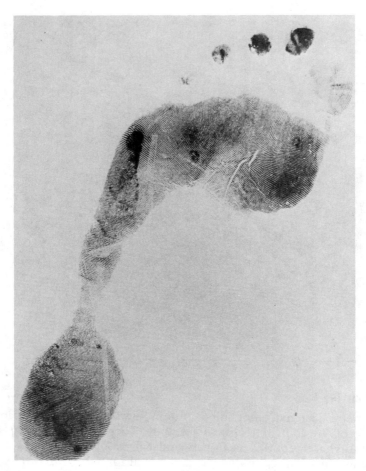

Figure 3.29 Sole print.

Like the palm, the sole is generally divided into a number of regions (Figure 3.30). The *hallucal* region corresponds to the distal thenar and first interdigital region of the palm. Whorl patterns are quite
common in this area and are usually quite large. The proximal *thenar*
area of the sole is seldom printed to any extent and is that area below
the hallucal region and to the inside of the midline of the foot. The
hypothenar region of the sole is below the hallucal region and to the
outside of the foot. Patterning may be present in this area [usually a
tibial (radial) loop], but because of the shape of the foot it is generally
not printed. The *calcar* region of the sole is the heel. Except for the
interdigital region, because of the shape of the foot, the ridges in a
sole print will be seen to cross the foot at approximately right angles
to the axis of the foot.

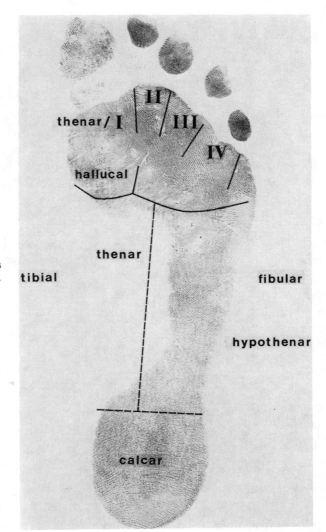

Figure 3.30 The regions and margins of the sole.

Although toes do possess patterning of the same type that is found in the fingers, they are seldom seen in forensic comparisons because of the curvature of the toes. Whorls are less common in toes than in fingers, whereas arches are more common.

Figure 3.30 shows an ordinary sole print with the designation of the various regions indicated. Figure 3.31 shows the same sole printed somewhat more extensively. Barely visible toward the fibular margin is a loop formation which has printed faintly because it is near the area where the friction ridged skin begins to give way to nonfriction ridged skin. It can be easily seen that a sole print taken by pressing

Figure 3.31 A more complete print of the same sole shown in Figure 3.30.

the foot against a flat surface leaves a large portion of the sole un-printed.

Just as palm prints are classified according to the location and types of patterns within the whole print, sole prints can be similarly classified. It can be seen in the print in Figures 3.29 and 3.30 that the interdigital area contains three whorls and a loop formation, each associated with a particular interdigital area. The sole print in Figure 3.29 shows only a single whorl and a loop pattern. On the basis of such pattern types and locations it is possible to classify, file, and search sole prints, just as finger and palm prints can be classified and filed.

The Evidence Print

4

Evidence prints are usually divided into three categories: latent prints, visible prints, and plastic impressions. These are convenient descriptors, as long as one bears in mind that they are not mutually exclusive and may not precisely describe the cause or appearance of any particular evidence print. An evidence print composed of a certain material may, on one substrate, be truly latent while an identically composed print on a different substrate may be quite visible. The plastic impression, when made in a material that is sufficiently soft and deep, will be seen as an excellent three-dimensional mold of the friction skin that made it. When shallow, however, the plastic impression will have virtually no three-dimensional aspect at all and may, in fact, be latent in the sense that some type of enhancement will be necessary before it can become visible and useful.

The term *latent print* is generally used to describe any type of print found at the scene of a crime or on evidence associated with a crime. While this practice may be useful from the standpoint of simplicity, it does tend to blur even more the distinctions between types of evidence prints which are already quite imprecise. A better term, which does not imply a causative factor for the print being considered, is *evidence print*, which is preferred by the author. It should not be construed to imply that such prints are related to only criminal matters: such prints (or impressions as the case may be) may be evidence of occupancy, possession, or presence not related to a criminal matter.

The Latent Print

The term *latent* means hidden or concealed. When applied to evidence prints it means that, in its original form, the print cannot be seen and must be developed or enhanced by some means to make it visible and subject to collection and comparison. For the most part, latent prints are composed of perspiration and body oils. Because these materials are colorless, or nearly so, and because the amount of the deposit is usually quite small, prints made of these materials are *usually* latent. Other materials, such as hair oil, hand cream, animal fat, or any body fluid may constitute the material deposited as a latent print.

A latent print may also be caused by the removal of material from a surface rather than the deposition of material. If the surface touched is covered by a moist or tacky substance that adheres to the friction ridges when they contact the surface, then a "negative" of the normally expected latent print can occur. Also, if the surface of interest is covered by a powdery substance or dust, it is possible for that material to adhere to the moist or tacky material on the skin so that, when the palm or finger is lifted, a negative print will be left.

Under the appropriate conditions, latent prints may be left on virtually any surface. These conditions are determined by the nature of the deposited or removed material, the nature and condition of the substrate, and the condition of the skin which is to remove some material coated on the substrate. The student can easily demonstrate that this is so by conducting a few very simple experiments.

One interesting demonstration requires the use of a piece of chromed or otherwise brightly plated metal and a container of water. First, clean the piece of chrome by polishing it well with a clean cloth and place it in the container of water. Then "oil" a finger by rubbing it beside the nose, or on the forehead. (If ones' complexion is quite dry it may be necessary to use another oily or greasy substance, such as butter, cooking oil, or animal fat.) Once the finger is well coated, simply immerse it and press on the submerged piece of metal. Then remove the object, shake off the excess water and allow it to air dry. Once the object is quite dry it can be processed to develop the latent print, or the latent print may be faintly visible without development due to the highly reflective surface of the chrome. The print may also be placed on the object before it is submerged. The latent print may survive while submerged for hours or days without affecting its quality when finally developed. Here the appropriate conditions consist of a very receptive surface and a print composed of a material that is not soluble in water.

Another demonstration, requiring a bit more preparation, is to take a piece of glass and smoke it by holding it over a burning cigarette or tobacco pipe until it is thinly coated with the tar in the smoke. The coating is then allowed to "set" for a day or two and then is touched with a clean *dry* finger. Examination of the print will reveal it to be either a print caused by a roughening of the tarry substance where it was contacted by the ridges, or the substance will have been removed by the ridges leaving a negative or tonally reversed print that may be developed with ordinary latent print powder and that will have clear ridges and dark furrows.

It is even possible to develop a latent print on ice (Figure 4.1). The only condition that must be observed to do this is that the ice must remain frozen at all times! First an ice cube is removed from the freezer, quickly touched and then returned. Some time later it is again removed and *very* quickly processed with "magnetic" powder, whereupon the print should develop. The print will have been caused by one of two mechanisms: either a deposit of material was placed on the ice when it was touched, or the surface of the ice was slightly thawed where contacted by the ridges which caused a change in the surface of the ice when refrozen. The point is that virtually anything can, under the appropriate conditions, retain a usable print.

As a practical matter, one is seldom likely to find usable prints on items that have been submerged or on ice cubes. There are so many variables involved in the leaving of the print, not to mention its remaining relatively undisturbed, that it is sometimes surprising that usable prints are found at all.

The Visible Print

Visible prints are, obviously, prints that can be seen without any enhancement being necessary. Often the only difference between a latent print and a visible print is the substrate on which they are placed: a print composed of a substance that would be quite invisible on a white wall may be easily seen if it is on a glass mirror. All of the conditions that affect the leaving of a latent print also affect the leaving of a visible print. Visible prints may be made of blood, perspiration, feces, motor oil, face cream, or any substance that contrasts sufficiently with the substrate.

On many surfaces a print may become visible with the proper lighting. Prints in dust, for instance, may be quite invisible until illuminated with oblique light. It may be appropriate, however, to consider the light to be an enhancement technique and such prints to be actually latent. This is a fine distinction to be sure, but it amply illustrates the difficulty that is often encountered in attempting to categorize evidence prints as to their "type."

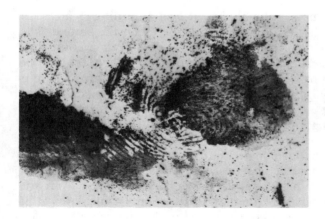

Figure 4.1 A latent print lifted from an ice cube after two days.

Using ordinary adhesive transparent tape it is possible to demonstrate the nature of prints that are visible with proper lighting but may not be seen otherwise. Merely touching the tape will produce the print to be examined. The print may be difficult or impossible to see under normal diffuse lighting conditions. But if held up to a light source and viewed by transmitted light, the print will be quite visible (Figure 4.2a). The print will also be easily seen with oblique lighting (Figure 4.2b). In this case the print is not caused by a transfer of material to or from the substrate, but rather by a disturbance of the otherwise smooth surface of the adhesive by contact with the friction ridges. This causes a change in the light-transmitting or -reflecting characteristics of the adhesive. Whether the print is to be called latent or visible is of no real importance; the only real concern is that it is there and is available for comparison.

The Plastic Impression

Plastic impressions are, generally, caused by touching some semisolid substance which is capable of retaining a three-dimensional representation of the friction ridges. The substance may be window glazing putty, soft wax, wet paint, grease, or any other substance that can be displaced by pressure from the ridges and which will not flow back to form a smooth surface. Because of their three-dimensional character, plastic impressions are usually visible (Figure 4.3); if an impression is very shallow, however, or if the substance is very dark or transparent, the impression may be difficult to see.

Plastic impressions, even if quite deeply impressed, are still fairly shallow: there is not a great deal of distance from the top of the ridge to the bottom of the valley. Such prints are therefore usually seen

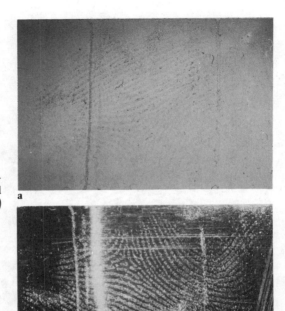

Figure 4.2 a. A print on transparent tape seen by transmitted light. b. The same print as in (a) as seen with oblique light.

only when the light is such that the deeper portions are in shadow. The shallower the impression the more oblique the lighting angle must be in order for the impressions to be seen. If the substance impressed is dark and dull, there may not be enough difference between shadow and highlight to detect the presence of the plastic impression readily. Plastic impressions in a transparent substance on an opaque surface may not be immediately apparent because of light transmission through the impressed substance causing the shadows in the depressions to be quite faint.

Different substances may be impressed under different conditions. Paint needs to be still fresh, or relatively so, if it is to take an impression. However, if it is quite wet and liquid, it may flow back after being touched, leaving no trace of the impression. Soft wax may readily be impressed but hard waxes must be heated and made soft. If a wax impression is reheated, the impression may be destroyed. Plastic impressions are generally as transient as any other type of evidence print and are subject to as many conditions for their existence.

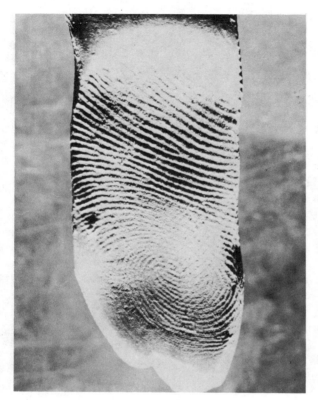

Figure 4.3 Plastic impression.

Locating, Developing, Preserving, and Collecting Evidence Prints

The development, collection, and preservation of evidence prints and impressions are preparatory steps to allow subsequent comparison of those prints and impressions to the known or exemplar prints. At times, these steps will be done very easily; at other times, the process may be quite complex and time consuming. *Development* is the process of making a print or impression visible and, in most cases, is also the equivalent of locating the print. *Preserving* the print is simply keeping the print in the best possible condition. *Collection*, which may or may not be the same as preservation, is the process of putting a print in a form that can be taken to the place where it will subsequently be compared.

The likelihood of developing usable evidence is certainly enhanced if one is aware of the nature of the print which is to be developed.

Latent prints are particularly bothersome since the very existence of such a print is rarely known until after a particular technique has been successful. Therefore, unfortunately, the searcher most often will have to rely on an assumption as to the nature of the material of which the print is composed. If the assumption is in error, the evidence print may be destroyed or the method selected may so mask the surface that, even if another technique could work properly, the results will not be visible.

The nature of the surface suspected of bearing an evidence is also useful information that can increase the likelihood of recovering the print. If the substrate responds to the developing agent along with the latent print material, the developed print may be completely masked. It is also possible for the substrate alone to respond to the developing agent, creating a masking effect that makes further attempts at development futile.

The combination of conditions that can cause a print to be made are so numerous that it is impractical to attempt to devise a set of rules that define a particular technique as the only appropriate technique for a particular surface. The best that can be done in this regard is to rely on the worker's ability to correlate information relating to the mechanisms of the various development techniques with the task at hand and to apply sound judgment in the selection of the developing agent.

In a sense it is perhaps fortunate that most latent prints must be assumed to be composed of perspiration and sebum (body oil). Barring some indication that this is not the case, a few easily mastered techniques will yield results that can be assumed to be optimal. These techniques fall into three very broad categories:

1. The addition of a colored agent that is expected to adhere differentially to, or be absorbed by, the latent print material (or the substrate).
2. The alteration of the composition of the latent print material so that it contrasts with the substrate.
3. The use of the difference (if any) in the reflectivity, or a natural color difference, between the latent print and the substrate. This generally involves the use of lighting and photography.

Before any attempt to develop latent prints is made, the object or surface should be carefully examined for visible prints. Because of the uncertainties involved in any development method, and the possibility of destruction or degradation of the prints if the method is not optimal, it is certainly desirable to consider locating and preserving or recording any visible prints or impressions before proceeding.

One method of examining a surface for prints is to take advantage of any difference in reflectivity between the latent print material and the substrate. By moving a strong light so that it reflects from different angles with respect to the surface and the observer, it is sometimes possible to detect the existence of prints that are otherwise invisible. Not finding prints with this technique does not, by any means, indicate that prints do not exist; it means only that none were seen.

When there is some question as to whether a particular method is capable of developing a latent print on a surface, it is possible to make a test print by placing one's own print on the surface and attempting to develop it. While this is certainly a useful practice, the worker should be aware that the results only apply to the ability of the method to develop a test print of known quality: to assume that the results of such a test will apply to the evidence prints sought is to assume that the test print and the evidence print are of the same composition and condition. It must also be assumed that the substrate is in the same condition over its entire surface since the surface condition and composition, as well as the presence or absence of contaminants can affect the development of a latent print by any particular technique.

There are many different ways to develop and preserve evidence prints and impressions. The technique used may depend on the physical properties of the latent print material or upon its chemical composition. Some techniques which depend upon the chemical composition of the latent print material are used only for substrate with specific characteristics. In fact, some techniques are even designed to act upon the substrate instead of the latent print. The following discussion of various development, collection, and preservation techniques is not intended to be complete; however, it will give the reader an understanding of the techniques most commonly used.

Powders

The use of various types of powder is, by far, the most common method of developing latent prints. Powders are used primarily on surfaces that are nonabsorbent so that the latent print material remains on, and is not absorbed into, the surface of the substrate. Powder develops latent prints when it adheres to the moist or tacky substance composing the latent print. The use of power is a relatively simple process and can be used successfully with very little practice, however, it can become quite complex as the circumstances surrounding the object to be processed, the nature of the object, and the composition of the latent print vary.

Selecting the powder. There are many different powders available from commercial sources for developing latent prints. These powders are compounded to have different characteristics to make them work better on different surfaces and to suit the personal requirements of the individual worker. Whatever the composition of the powder, its purpose is to adhere to the latent print and not to the substrate. The test of the appropriateness of a particular powder is whether the user is able to use it successfully for the task at hand.

It is certainly possible for the worker to compound powders that are quite serviceable and possibly even superior to those that are obtained commercially. Excellent formulas are available in various publications[15, 16] (Olsen, 1978; Moenssens, 1970) and the reader is encouraged to experiment, or at least be familiar with some of these. Caution should be exercised both in compounding and in using any powder because some of the ingredients used are known to be hazardous if ingested or inhaled; even the nontoxic ingredients can be irritating to some individuals.

Powders can be obtained or made in many different colors, though black and gray are the colors most commonly used. Other colors, such as red, yellow, orange, and white, are also available in order to give maximum contrast with the color of the substrate.

Black powders give the most consistently good results since they have the least tendency to "paint" or adhere to the substrate as well as to the latent print material. While it is useful to make test prints with any powder, it is highly recommended if the powder is one of the colored varieties because of their increased tendency to paint. Black powder will also contrast well with many substrates, regardless of color, due to differences in reflectivity between the powder and the substrate. It is even possible to use black powder effectively on a black surface if it is not the same dull black as the powder; it is even possible to photograph such prints (Figure 4.4). Since any prints collected are most likely to be compared to record prints that are black on a white background, it is preferable, if possible, to produce evidence prints with the same tonal values.

There will be times, of course, when a gray or colored powder will seem preferable to black powder, as when a colored surface is quite dark and dull or when there is some question whether the print can be successfully lifted with tape. In such a circumstance it may be advisable to photograph the latent print in situ, in which case maximum contrast of the latent print to the substrate must be sought. If the surface being processed is, say, dark blue, a yellow powder may be indicated. The yellow powder may contrast very well with the blue surface, but if the print is lifted and placed on a white or black backing, it may be quite faint and difficult to see and compare. Cau-

Figure 4.4 Latent print developed with black powder on a black surface.

tion should therefore be exercised and the method of collection and preservation considered along with the color of powder.

It is the author's experience that the use of powders other than black is seldom indicated. Most surfaces can be successfully processed with black powder and the print preserved by lifting with tape and placing it on a card. Only if there is substantial question as to the efficacy of black powder are other colors considered; even then the surface is tested with that powder first to determine the painting and contrast characteristics of the powder.

Surfaces that are suitable for processing with powders include glass, metal, most painted surfaces, and plastics. Some papers are also included: many paper items are plastic coated or otherwise treated for attractiveness or resistance to moisture; such items should not be overlooked when processing with powder. If there is a question as to whether the surface is absorbent, the item can be tested with some expectation, though not certainty, of accuracy by making a test print, waiting for an hour or two, and then applying the powder.

Special powders. Many different types of powder have been developed for special purposes. With *fluorescent powders*, which are used much like ordinary powders but fluoresce brightly under ultraviolet (UV) illumination, it is possible to photograph a print and be assured

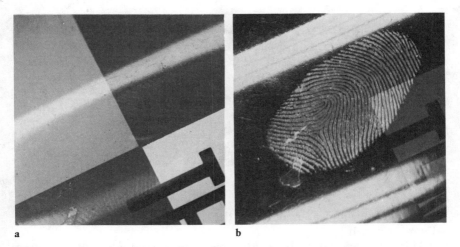

a   b

Figure 4.5 a. Latent print on multicolored surface. **b.** The same latent print, developed with fluorescent powder and photographed with UV light.

of a reasonable record regardless of the color or the number of colors of the substrate (Figure 4.5). This is certainly a useful material to have available but there are some constraints to its use. First, it must be determined that the item or substrate being processed does not also fluoresce with UV light. Secondly, because these powders are very light in color, it is difficult to know when a print develops unless the processing is done under UV light. This requires the ability to exclude other light (darken the room) during both processing and photography. Because UV light can damage the eyes, care should be taken to wear proper eye protection when using this type of material.

"Magnetic" powders, which are not actually magnetic, are ferrous powders applied with a magnetic wand. The magnet in the wand holds the powders in long rays which are pulled across the surface being processed (Figure 4.6). If there is something on the surface, or if the surface itself holds the particles with sufficient force to overcome the magnetic attraction, the particles will remain on the surface. Just as with ordinary powders, these depend upon the print being on, not in, the surface. If the print has been absorbed by the substrate, such as a piece of paper, little success can be expected. Though these powders come in black and gray, even the black is comparatively light in color; some workers add a small amount of ordinary black powder to the ferrous powder to increase its density or blackness.

These powders can be especially useful on such items as finished leather and rough plastics, where the minute texture of the surface has a tendency to capture particles of ordinary powder. Ferrous powders should not be used on ferrous articles because of the tendency of

Figure 4.6 Ferrous powder and magnetic wand.

the magnetic wand to magnetize the surface, causing the powder to adhere everywhere.

"Magnetic" powders have also been suggested for use on paper items that have been wet (Stone and Metzger, 1981). The successful use of these powders for this purpose depends, of course, on there being an oily or waxy latent print deposit at the surface of the paper to which the powder will adhere. Use of these powders has also been suggested for use in processing bodies for latent prints (Guttierrez, 1978). Here, the reader will recognize that it will be necessary to photograph any latent prints so developed because of the potential interference to a usable lift that could be caused by the texture of the skin the print is developed on. Similarly, many of the other surfaces for which such powders are suited may also require the use of photography to record prints developed because of their texture and the difficulties associated with using tape to "lift" prints from those surfaces.

There are other powders specially compounded to be used on metallic surfaces which, because of the minute texture or roughness of the unfinished metal, present special problems. These powders should be used cautiously and sparingly as they usually have a tendency to paint even the surfaces for which they were compounded. The older formulations tend to be metallic with large particle sizes. Powders of aluminum, bronze, copper and lead oxides have been used. While still used quite successfully by some, their use requires a substantial amount of practice if they are to be used successfully. They are also usually brightly colored so that they can be photographed easily: the rough surfaces for which they are used make lifting with tape less than certain.

A more recently developed powder is compounded to appear dark against a light substrate, and light on a dark substrate. Thus, though appearing light on a dark surface, when the print is lifted it can be preserved on a white card and appear dark (Figure 4.7). While it is unlikely to replace any of the ordinary powders, it is very useful on

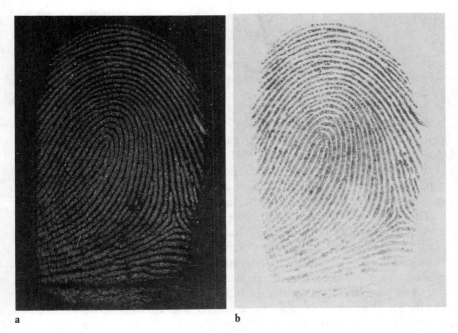

a   b

Figure 4.7 a. Latent print developed with Bi-Chromic® (Lightning Powder Co.) on a black surface. **b.** The same print lifted and placed on a white card.

multicolored surfaces as well as on dull neutral surfaces, where it is difficult to determine before processing just what color powder would provide the best working contrast.

Which powder to use in a particular circumstance is, as often as not, a matter of preference based upon experience. It is seldom possible to select the proper powder with precision. Powders may even be of the same color and yet differ in characteristics, due to different compositions. Homemade powders may vary from batch to batch even though containing the same ingredients. Similarly, latent prints vary in characteristics: some are quite liquid, others more dry; some are oily, and others are primarily water. The quality of the substrate, including even its electrical properties (static electricity can attract or repel powder particles and affect different powders to varying degrees), can affect the results of the processing. Since it is seldom, if ever, that all of these factors are known, the worker must rely on experience and, if necessary, make test prints.

Powder application methods. Once a powder has been selected it must be applied to the surface suspected to bear latent prints, on which, hopefully, it will adhere. Powder can be (a) brushed on with any of a number of types of brushes; (b) blown on with a bulb-type blower or even a spray can; or (c) poured on and blown or shaken off. The most common method of application is with a brush of some sort. The other methods are more suited to those circumstances where the use of a brush, no matter how soft, would cause the powder to paint or pack into the surface, or where the latent print is expected to be extremely fine and delicate.

As in the selection of powders, a method of application is appropriate if it works. Even if blowing or shaking powder across a surface does not develop prints, the use of a brush should still be considered: it is quite possible for a good latent print to have too little tack or be a bit too dry for powder to adhere without the force of a brush pushing the powder particles into the latent print material.

There are many types of brush that can be used effectively. Fiberglass, carbon filament, "camel" hair or sable, and feather are all currently available for application of powders (Figure 4.8). The fiberglass filament brush is the most commonly used brush now, having replaced the natural bristle brush because it is softer, holds more powder, and can cover a larger area with less work. The carbon filament brush has the same general characteristics as the fiberglass brush, but is perhaps a bit softer and has more fibers in the same size bundle.

Fiberglass and carbon filament brushes are more easily cleaned than natural bristle or feather brushes, which must be effectively dry cleaned using acetone or a similar solvent. It is necessary to clean any brush occasionally as it will inevitably become contaminated by oil or some similarly sticky substance, causing the filaments to stick together or contaminate the surface being processed.

Feather-duster-type brushes are intended for use on large areas and were in vogue when natural bristle brushes were the best available. Since the advent of the fiberglass and now the carbon filament brush, feather dusters have little practical value: large areas can be easily processed with the more modern and durable brushes.

The characteristics of the natural bristle brushes that have caused its general replacement by synthetic fiber brushes are, at times, advantageous. Because they do not carry a great deal of powder, natural bristle brushes are very useful for applying powders that have a tendency to paint, allowing greater control over the amount of powder applied. They are also good in circumstances where the texture of the substrate might tend to capture powder: the stiffer bristles allow excess powder to be more easily removed from the surface. There are also times when the development of a print depends upon the powder "packing" or being captured by a dry, rough deposit such as blood or even very old ordinary latent prints; in such cases the stiffer natural bristle brushes can again be used to good advantage.

Figure 4.8 Various
types of brush.

An interesting self-contained device that is available consists of a
fiberglass filament brush attached to a hollow handle, at the top of
which is a plastic bottle of powder (Figure 4.8). The brush can be
charged with powder from the bottle or retracted and capped for car-
rying in a pocket.

The type of brush selected is also, for the most part, a matter of
personal preference. The author prefers to use synthetic filament
brushes for most work but uses natural bristle brushes for most colored powders (other than black), or on such surfaces as unpainted or
lightly varnished wood, lightly oiled metal objects such as guns, or
where the enhancement of the latent print depends upon the physical
capturing of powder by a dried substance, rather than being developed
by powder sticking to a moist or tacky substance. One should gain
some experience through practice with the various brushes and powders to determine a preference and to develop a "feel" for the materials that will be used.

Collection and preservation of developed prints. A latent print that
has been developed can be (a) collected by lifting with an adhesive or
similar substance; (b) preserved by leaving it untouched on the surface or by coating or covering it and keeping the object on which it
appears; and/or (c) recorded by photography. It is even possible to do
all three.

Photography, which will be discussed in greater detail later on, is
very important to anyone working with evidence prints. When the
object bearing the print cannot be kept (or kept conveniently) or when
a print may be damaged by adhesive lifting, photography can be ab-
solutely critical. Even a mediocre photograph of a latent print is better than no print at all.

Preserving a latent print is certainly a simple concept. If the print is on an object that can be carried to where comparison will take place, then preservation is a viable technique. The object may be of any size from quite small to as large as a door, provided it can be transported without damaging the print. At times the print may be suspected to be composed of some substance that requires removal of the object to the laboratory for special development techniques. It may be somewhat cumbersome, however, to work with a developed latent print preserved on a door or on a section of wall. Fortunately this is seldom necessary if the print can be lifted or photographed. Chemical development techniques, which will be discussed later, are responsible for most situations requiring preservation of the object bearing the developed prints.

Care should be exercised if preserving powder-developed latent prints. Such prints are as delicate and as subject to damage as the undeveloped latent print. Also, if the substance composing the latent print should evaporate (as perspiration will), the powder may no longer adhere to the surface and may be lost. If it is necessary to maintain a print on the surface, it can be preserved by taping over it, or by applying a few light coats of clear lacquer or varnish. If this is to be done, the coating spray should be tested for its effect on the surface bearing the developed print and for its effect on the print itself: some prints, especially those developed with light-colored powders, may seemingly disappear into a clear shellac or lacquer.

Adhesive lifting is, by far, the most common method of putting a developed latent print in a form that can be transported and compared. There are a number of different materials devised for this purpose (Figure 4.9) and, like the selection of powder and brush, their use is a matter of preference. Lifting materials commonly used are clear or "frosted" 1–2-inch-wide tape, individual pieces of adhesive-coated clear acetate attached to black, white, or clear acetate, and adhesive-coated rubber lifters.

The most commonly used material is the clear or frosted tape, which is very much like ordinary adhesive tape. Although ordinary adhesive tape can be used, tape marketed as fingerprint lift tape is usually manufactured so that the adhesive is very smooth and will not impart any additional texture to the appearance of the lifted print. Use of these transparent tapes is convenient because the length is easily selected and strips can be easily overlapped if the developed print is too wide for a single one. Caution should be exercised when using frosted tape: if the developed print is very faint, or if gray or colored powders are used, frosted tape can reduce the effective contrast of the lifted print. This problem seldom occurs, however, and frosted tape has the additional advantage of reducing unwanted reflections.

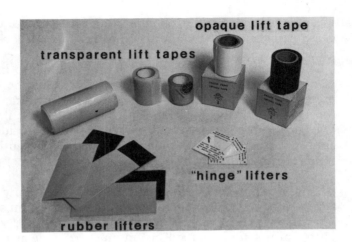

Figure 4.9 Various types of lifting material.

After making the lift, lifting tape is adhered to *lift cards*, which should have a very smooth surface; a rough surface can affect the definition of the lifted print. These lift cards should be available in black and white in order to contrast effectively with various colors of powder. It is also useful to have available some clear transparent material for times when there is some uncertainty about which color lift card would be most appropriate.

Hinge-style lifters are useful and come in a variety of sizes. While easy to use, the smaller sizes are useful for only small prints and do not provide much area for writing identifying information, such as a diagram of the location and orientation of the latent print on the object before lifting. If these materials are used, it is recommended that only the larger sizes be used—not only because of the additional room available for identifying information, but also because they are easier to manipulate when making comparisons.

One of the most enduring materials for lifting latent prints is the *rubber lifter*. This is simply a thin piece of black or white rubber with adhesive on one side. After lifting a print, a clear piece of acetate is placed over it to protect it. For general use these lifters would present one particular problem: because the adhesive is on an opaque material, the lifted prints is reversed, left to right, from the normal viewing position. This can be overcome by photographic techniques or by the experience of the examiner who makes the comparison. Many workers prefer this material for lifting prints from complex surfaces such as door knobs or items with deeply impressed designs because it stretches better than the tapes, which have a tendency to fold or buckle when used on such surfaces. Even so, care must be exercised when using rubber lifters on complex surfaces: too much tension can cause parts of the lifter already in place to break loose, to the detriment of the print.

The author's preference is to use frosted tape to lift a powder-developed print, unless another lift material would be better suited or preservation of the print on the object or by photography is necessary. Most prints can be successfully lifted with little, if any, difficulty. Evidence prints so lifted and properly marked for identification are easily transported, filed, and compared, and the author has had no trouble with their admissability in any court.

Using the powder development method. Before any item or surface is processed with powder some preliminary steps must be performed. The first is, of course, to examine the surface for visible prints. If visible prints are found a decision must be made as to how they will be treated. Photography may be indicated or the prints may require enhancement before further collection, preservation, or recording is possible.

If no visible prints are seen, or if it is decided to enhance such prints, it is necessary to determine if powder is the most appropriate development. If the object or surface is nonabsorbent the technique of choice is almost always the use of powder and brush. Selection of the particular powder and brush combination is, as has been stated, a matter of personal preference; however, unless some particular condition indicates some other combination is necessary, a good commercial black powder and synthetic fiber brush will usually work as well as any.

The brush should be free of contaminants such as oil or grease and it should not have been used with a different color of powder than that to be used. The powder used should be dry, loose, and free of debris that may be introduced by previous work or by collecting and saving powder from the work counter. The brush is charged by dipping the tips of the bristles into the powder and shaking or tapping the excess powder from the brush. If too much powder is on the brush, the job becomes somewhat messier than necessary, and excess powder dropping on the work reduces the amount of control the worker can exercise over the development process.

The charged brush is then gently moved over the surface being processed. Only the tips of the bristles should touch the surface: abrasion from the brush could damage the latent prints. If some area seems to collect powder it should be examined to determine if the powder is adhering to a print. If so, the area should be brushed until the print seems to have reached maximum contrast with the background. If a natural bristle brush is used, the print should be brushed in the direction of the flow of the ridges as much as possible, once the ridge structure of the print becomes apparent; as soft as the natural bristle brush is, it is still quite stiff enough to be abrasive to the delicate substance of the latent print. Synthetic fiber brushes are much less abrasive and so following the ridge flow is not critical, but it can do no harm.

It is entirely possible for an apparently still-developing latent print to suddenly disappear. This is probably due to the latent print material being completely absorbed into the powder and having little adhesion to the substrate. This can happen on any surface, though it seems to occur most often on bright chrome and metal foils. Although the student can be cautioned to not "overprocess" a print, there is no certain way to judge the point at which a print has reached optimum density. A better piece of advice is perhaps to not be quite so demanding for density and clarity of a latent print: the point in processing where a print becomes useful for comparison is the point at which it should be collected or preserved.

Of course, not all latent prints develop cleanly with little or no background: quite often a print will develop as lines barely darker than the background which has also collected powder. Such prints can certainly be useful for comparison purposes. Often, however, a second, third, or even fourth lift of the print may be clearer than the previous ones due to the background being cleaned by being lifted along with the powder adhering to it (Figure 4.10). At times the first lift may show no evidence of a print at all, the density of the background equalling the density of the print, whereas a subsequent lift may be quite good. Whether such a print should be procesed between lifts is a matter of judgment. Generally, if after the first lift the print appears to have reasonable density against a light background, it is probably best to lift again without further processing. If the latent print is quite delicate, or not well adhered to the substrate, the additional processing may damage it.

The material composing a latent print can, over time or under rigorous conditions, dry to the point that powder will not adhere to it as it does to a "normal" latent print. If the deposit composing such a print is sufficiently rough or raised from the substrate, it is possible for the powder to enhance it anyway due to its packing against the sides of the ridges or by becoming trapped in the minute roughness of the print. Lifts of such prints are usually quite faint; sometimes so faint that they cannot be seen on the lift.

Dry prints can sometimes be restored by adding moisture to the latent print material. This can be done in a humidity chamber or simply by breathing on the print. Breathing also warms the latent print material which, if sebum or a similar substance, will soften and allow

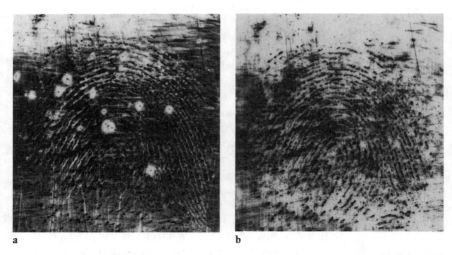

a   b

Figure 4.10 a. Latent print obscured by powder adhering to the background. **b.** Second lift of the same latent print.

powder to adhere to it. If this is done, care should be taken to allow any moisture condensed on the substrate to evaporate; otherwise, disaster could result. Warming the latent print with the work light is also useful.

The color density of the lifted print depends upon the quantity of powder that adheres to the adhesive of the lift. It is possible to improve a lift by warming the tape, by using the work light or hand, after it has been placed on the developed print. This softens the adhesive and allows it to be pressed down to trap or adhere to more of the powder particles. This can help produce a better lift of some faintly developed latent prints.

Once the print has been satisfactorily developed, a decision must be made to lift, preserve, or photograph (record) it. Unless a print is inaccessible to a camera, it can be photographed as well as lifted or preserved. Also, if the print is substantial enough to survive the lifting process, all three procedures can be used. Some jurisdictions or agencies may require that the print be preserved or at least photographed in situ. Unless these restrictions obtain, or if something may interfere with collection by lifting, lifting is the most convenient technique and is recommended by the author.

The lifting material to be used is the one with which the worker feels most comfortable and finds the most convenient. Some thought should be given to the preference of the person who will ultimately have to work with the lifted print, but the first priority is recovery of the print: if use of an unfamiliar material causes a print to be damaged or poorly lifted, then there may be nothing to compare anyway.

It has been suggested that, when using any lift material, the adhesive be adhered first at the center of the best part of the print and then pressed in a widening circle until the print is fully covered. This is a good technique and, on complex surfaces, can ensure that the lifting medium will not buckle and fold over the best part of the latent print. On flat surfaces the author prefers to adhere the tape or lift at one side of the area to be lifted and then press the tape across the developed print. Simply laying the lifting material down and then pressing it into contact is one of the primary causes of "fish eyes" or air bubbles under the tape.

Air bubbles under the lifting medium can prevent contact between the adhesive and the print, as can small bits of grit. Before removing a lift from the surface, it should be examined for such areas and pressed into good contact. For this purpose, the eraser on an ordinary pencil is a good aid. Air bubbles are a common occurrence when taping prints on plastic objects, apparently due to the electrical properties of the material causing a repulsion of the tape by a similar static charge on the substrate. This same condition can cause loose particles of charged powder to be attracted to the tape, obscuring the print being lifted or, worse, acting as a barrier between the tape and the substrate which allows the tape to slide across the surface. This problem is most prevalent during periods of very low humidity.

Static neutralizing devices, available as photographic darkroom aids or for general laboratory use, can help to mitigate this problem. These devices operate either on line current, with batteries, or with piezoelectric crystals. A device of this type that does not require contact with the surface being neutralized is recommended.

Even though the tape or other lifting medium has certain dimensions it is not necessary that it retain them. Trimming the material to fit the object or a depression can allow successful lifting of a print from a difficult location. The tape can be cut, holed, rolled into tubes, or even tacked down and the processed object pressed to it. How a print is lifted is less important than its being lifted successfully.

If a developed latent print is on a complex surface such as the shoulder of a bottle or a doorknob, it is still possible to make a good lift if the limitations of the lifting material are respected. Even rubber lifters are limited in how sharply they may bend in more than one direction at the same time. If good control is exercised over the material, it is possible to maintain but a narrow band of contact between the lifter and the surface; by pulling up on one end as fresh adhesive is pressed into place, relatively large prints can be lifted from surfaces that are essentially round (Figure 4.11).

a

Figure 4.11 Latent prints may be lifted from complex curved surfaces. **a.** Light bulb with latent print around the circumference. **b.** Lift of a latent print from the light bulb.

b

Occasionally, latent prints may develop on small cylindrical objects, such as firearms cartridge cases. The entire circumference of such an object can be lifted by securing a large enough piece of lift material, adhesive side up, to a piece of cardboard. The arrangement is then secured to the work surface. The item, handled carefully by the edges, is placed on the adhesive with an area bearing the least or poorest ridge detail contacting the adhesive first, and is then rolled along the adhesive. It is helpful if the lifting material is backed by a

a   b

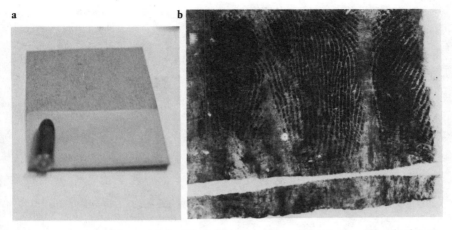

Figure 4.12 Latent prints may be lifted from the circumference of small cylinders. **a.** Beginning the lift from a revolver cartridge. **b.** The resultant lifted latent print.

few layers of tissue paper or similar material; this provides some give to the lift material to ensure full contact of the object with the adhesive (Figure 4.12). If a cartridge has a rim at the base, it can be placed over the edge of the cardboard. Many times it will be found that imagination is as important as knowledge of a "standard" technique.

Iodine

The use of iodine is a time-honored technique for developing latent prints and is effective on virtually any surface. Iodine develops latent prints by being absorbed into the oily substance of the latent print, assuming that it has an oily composition (Figure 4.13). Regardless of the particular method of application, the mechanism of development is to cause metallic iodine to *sublime* (go directly from the solid state to the gas state) and expose the object being processed to the "fumes." However used, great care must be exercised, since iodine in any form is toxic. In very low concentrations, iodine is used medicinally; in the concentrations used for latent print development, it can cause damage to mucous membranes.

There are a number of "standard" methods for applying iodine. One that is portable and can be used on large objects uses a blowpipe device (Figure 4.14). There are now devices marketed that use electric blowers to force heated air through the pipe to sublime the iodine. If a blowpipe is to be used at all, it is this kind that is recommended: it

Figure 4.13 Iodine-developed latent print.

minimizes contact with the device and causes more efficient sublimation of the iodine than blowing with the mouth. Also, calcium carbonate used to dry the breath can quickly become waterlogged, increasing the effort necessary to blow. If allowed to sit for a while after use, calcium carbonate can dry and harden and become very difficult to remove from the pipe.

Another method, suitable for small objects, uses a cabinet device. The object is placed in the cabinet and a heater of some sort, often an electric light bulb, heats and sublimes the iodine, filling the cabinet with fumes. This type of device should be used in a well ventilated area: when the cabinet is opened, volumes of sublimed iodine will escape into the vicinity of the worker. This gas will return to the metallic state quite quickly when removed from the heat source and will deposit on any surface.

Iodine captured in glass beads is a commercially available form that is quite easily used. Useful for small objects, the beads are poured on

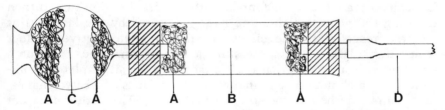

Figure 4.14 Iodine fuming pipe. Constructed primarily of laboratory glassware, the noted components are (**A**) glasswool, (**B**) calcium carbonate, (**C**) metallic iodine, and (**D**) 12–18 in. "neoprene" or rubber tube.

the surface and shaken or brushed over the surface. The surface must, of course, be flat and horizontal.

Latent prints developed with iodine are a brownish color, which tends to limit the usefulness of this process for light-colored surfaces. Iodine-developed prints are also transient unless "fixed" by some means; this can be an advantage, as when a paper item must be examined without leaving any indication of the item having been processed. If this is to be done, it should be done carefully: iodine may stain the surface processed.

Generally, latent prints that will develop with iodine will also develop with other, less transitory materials. If the surface bearing the print is nonabsorbent, the oily material will almost certainly develop with powder. On absorbent surfaces other chemicals can be used that produce prints that are somewhat more lasting. If there is any advantage to the use of iodine it is that it is not detrimental to any other processing technique and can, therefore, be used to locate areas to be processed by other methods. It must be remembered that iodine is absorbed by oily substances without regard to whether it is developing a latent print. Also, if the print does not have much oily content, the lack of development with iodine does not mean that no prints are present.

Iodine-developed prints can be "fixed" by the application of a 1% solution of starch in water applied by spraying. The print will turn blue and can be expected to last for several weeks to several months. The starch can also be brushed on as a powder and then subjected to steam as suggested by Larson (1962). A patented fixing method (Trowell, 1975) is to treat the developed print with a 0.2% solution of tetrabase in 1,1,2-trichlorotrifluorethane, after which it will turn blue-green. Somewhat simpler, though not as lasting, is to treat the print with water as a spray or as steam: the print turns bluish and is more stable than if untreated, but is not long lasting enough to be called permanent for practical purposes.

Iodine-developed prints can be lifted from many surfaces by pressing a silver plate into firm contact with the developed print and then exposing the plate to light. The iodine captured by the latent print material reacts with the silver, forming a photoreactive product which turns dark. To be successful the latent print needs to be on a fairly smooth surface so that the contact with the silver plate is complete. This technique is possible to use when it is suspected that latent prints may be on a person (Adcock, 1977). The author does not recommend that live persons be subjected to iodine fuming and it is the author's experience that latent prints that may develop on a corpse with iodine will also develop with magnetic or even ordinary powder techniques.

Ninhydrin (1,2-Triketohydrindantine Monohydrate)

Ninhydrin is a chemical that is used in the biological sciences to indicate the presence of amino acids. Amino acids, present in perspiration and other exudates, are deposited in latent print material and can be developed by the application of ninhydrin (see Figure 5.4, p. 116). Prints developed with ninhydrin may vary from bluish purple to almost red in color.

Ninhydrin can be applied by dipping, brushing, or spraying the item being processed. Because it is applied in liquid form, ninhydrin is used on porous or absorbent surfaces. Once applied to the surface, the solution is allowed to evaporate and, if the worker is in no hurry, the latent prints can be expected to be developed fully in 2–3 days. Under humid and warm conditions, prints may begin to develop within a few minutes; conversely, if the ambient temperature and humidity are low, the development may take a week or so. The author has experienced prints developing a number of weeks after the processing.

The ninhydrin reaction can be accelerated by the application of heat, as in an oven, although the prints will generally be quite red and spotty. Moist heat will develop the prints to a more purple hue and the ridges will be more complete. The use of an ordinary household steam iron has proved to be quite adequate in the author's work, although it is possible to construct heat and humidity chambers. If an iron is used, it should not be allowed to touch the work but should be held about half an inch above it. An oven should not be so hot as to char or scorch the work (70–80°C is usually adequate) and, if possible, control the humidity to about 80% relative humidity. The worker should avoid getting any condensation or water drops on the work as the reaction product is water soluble.

Ninhydrin crystals can be dissolved in acetone, alcohol, or petroleum ether for use: 3–5g/l is adequate. The author prefers the lower concentration to control any background reaction that may occur.

Additional applications of the reagent are possible if the developed prints are faint or if nothing develops after the first application.

The ordinary solvents mentioned can be quite dangerous due to toxicity and flash-point characteristics; hence, the author prefers a ninhydrin solution that uses liquid freon as the working solute. A stock solution is first made by adding 100 ml of ethanol and 25g of ninhydrin crystals. While stirring, slowly add 50 ml of glacial acetic acid. The mixture must be stirred until the ninhydrin is completely dissolved. This stock solution has a shelf life of many months if stored in a tightly stoppered bottle in a cool location.

The working solution is made by adding 30–35 ml stock solution to 1000 ml freon (1,2,2-trichlorotrifluorethane). This must be stirred until fully mixed. It often occurs that even after long, vigorous stirring, small globules of the stock solution remain on top of the mixture; these can be removed if the mixture is poured through a good-quality filter paper into the storage bottle. The loss of a small quantity of the stock solution in this way has very little effect on the strength of the working solution.

Because there is so little alcohol in the working solution and because freon has no effect on most inks, the solution is quite suitable for all types of documents. This is a definite advantage over the use of other solvents such as acetone and ether. Before any freon is used, however, it should be tested for its effect on inks anyway, as any contaminants it may contain could cause inks to run. The working solution has a shelf life of at least three months if stored in a tightly stoppered bottle in a cool location.

Freon is highly volatile and should be used only in well ventilated areas. If exposed to open flame it also may produce toxic gases. Acetone, petroleum ether, and alcohol must also be used in well ventilated areas and any source of flame or potentially spark-producing devices (such as light switches) should be disabled.

The prints developed by ninhydrin on absorbent surfaces are actually in the substrate and the clarity of the developed print is affected by the texture of the surface. Very fibrous papers may so obscure the print developed that it will be difficult or impossible to distinguish the minutiae. Also, the color of the developed print and the fact that the print is not opaque can make it difficult or impossible to see on some colored surfaces. When this is a potential problem is may be necessary to use a different method of development.

Ninhydrin-developed prints are generally stable and can be expected to persist for many months, although the author has experienced some prints fading substantially in a matter of a few weeks or months, primarily when the original reaction was quite weak. It is also the author's experience that prints developed on "no-carbon-required" paper, such as is commonly used for carbonless copies of forms, are more likely to fade than others. If the worker has any doubt as to the durability of a particular print, photography can be used to record the print.

Ninhydrin-developed prints are subject to a small degree of enhancement by the application of additional reagents (Reed, 1980, 1981). The enhancement consists of minor color changes and not necessarily intensification of the developed print. Nickel nitrate and zinc chloride, 1% in alcohol, will cause a color change to red or orange, respectively. Selenium sulfide (available as a toner for photographs) diluted with about 30 parts alcohol will cause a color change to brown. The solvents used will cause most inks to run, so the application should be made with a spray device capable of delivering a very small droplet size.

Prints developed with ninhydrin can be "fixed" by an application of commercially available solutions of a copper salt. The solution is green and also causes a small color change in the developed print. If the print is quite faint, the application of the solution, which also stains the substrate, may obscure the print. The solution will also run many inks.

It is also possible for some substrates to react with ninhydrin, so a spot test may be in order. For instance, it is the author's practice to avoid any attempts to accelerate the ninhydrin reaction on paper currency: The application of heat almost invariably causes a very strong background reaction that is too intense to allow latent prints to be seen.

para-Dimethylaminocinnimaldehyde (PDMAC)

PDMAC is a highly sensitive chemical that reacts with urea present in perspiration to form an intense red color. The resultant print is easily recorded with orthochromatic film if the background was initially white or light colored (Figure 4.15). The solution must be acidic to work and is pH-dependant; therefore, if the substrate is highly alkaline, a more acidic solution may be required than is usual.

A working solution for PDMAC suggested by the FBI is to dissolve 2.5 g PDMAC in 500 ml acetone to make one solution, and then dissolve 7.5 g toluene sulfonic acid in a similar volume of acetone. Equal volumes of the two solutions are then mixed for use. Freon may also be used to replace the acetone if the PDMAC and toluence sulfonic acid are dissolved in small quantities of ethanol (much as ninhydrin is made to a stock solution). This freon solution is, of course, nonflammable and does not run most inks as does acetone. The solution is applied with an atomizer.

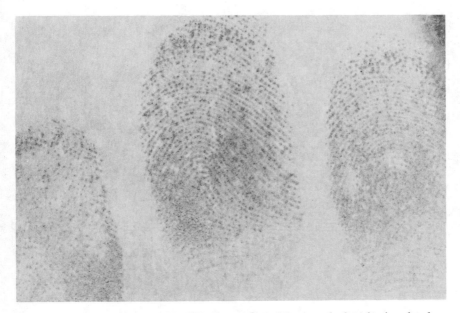

Figure 4.15 Latent prints developed with PDMAC. (Photographed 24 h after development, the prints had already begun to diffuse.)

While suitable for use on most types of paper, this reagent is not as certain to develop latent prints as is ninhydrin. It is also somewhat more difficult to control due to its dependence on pH. The high acidity of the solution may also be destructive to some substrates over time; developed prints should not be considered to be permanent for practical purposes and should be photographed if there is some indication that they will be needed more than a few weeks into the future.

Because it is very sensitive, solutions of PDMAC should be applied in a very fine spray. Generally, just barely wet the surface; multiple applications may be made without harm if the first spraying is unsuccessful. Latent prints usually develop without assistance in a few minutes and may develop immediately.

Silver Nitrate

Silver nitrate, used for developing latent prints on porous substrates such as wood, paper, and cloth, reacts with the sodium chloride deposited in perspiration to form silver chloride. The silver chloride is photoreactive and darkens on exposure to light (Figure 4.16).

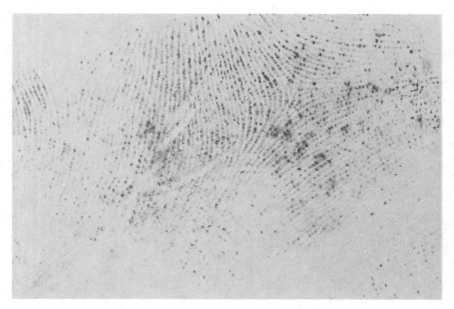

Figure 4.16 Latent print developed with silver nitrate on paper.

The object being processed can be sprayed, brushed, or dipped into the silver nitrate solution. It is then blotted to remove excess solution and allowed to air-dry. Prints will develop if the object is left in ordinary room light, but the development can be accelerated by exposing the object to a light source that is rich in ultraviolet light, such as a UV lamp or sunlight.

Because silver nitrate reacts with salt, any salt present in the substrate will also react and may obscure any developed latent. Even if the amount of salt in the substrate is quite low, excessive exposure to light can eventually cause the background to develop, obscuring what was at first a usable latent print. Prints developed with silver nitrate should be stored in a manner that prevents unnecessary exposure to light and heat.

The silver nitrate solution may be in distilled water or alcohol and a 3% solution is generally adequate: if too strong, excessive background reaction may result; if too weak, the solution may be below threshold level. Use of water as a solvent may cause problems because of the long time involved for drying; for this reason the author prefers to use ethanol. Caution must be exercised with either if inks are present on the substrate, not only because of the potential for destruction of handwriting evidence but because the running or diffusing ink may obscure any developed latent print.

Latent prints developed with silver nitrate are generally a brownish color. The developed ridges may appear as a dot pattern, with the dots representing the location of the pores. The prints are not permanent and will probably blur or be overcome by background reaction over a period of time even if carefully stored in light-tight packaging in a cool area. Therefore, if it is expected that there will be a substantial period of time during which the developed prints will need to be available, or if the print is quite faint, or if the substrate reacts more than minimally, the print should be recorded photographically.

Silver nitrate can also be used to develop latent prints on brass surfaces. This is primarily of concern when processing firearm ammunition (Figure 4.17). The object is immersed in the silver nitrate solution for a few seconds until a brownish material covers the surface. It is then gently washed or swabbed with cotton to remove the brownish substance, and developed latent prints appear dark against the lighter brass background. Prints so developed are very long lasting if the item is well rinsed to remove any excess silver nitrate. This technique is primarily suited to brass that has oxidized.

Since the silver nitrate development of latent prints is basically a photochemical reaction, photographic chemistry can be used to speed up the development of the latent print, and even make it permanent. The use of any standard photographic developer for paper will cause any latent prints that would develop with silver nitrate to be fully developed almost immediately upon application. Before such appli-

Figure 4.17 Latent print developed with silver nitrate on a brass cartridge case.

cation, however, the processed item must be thoroughly rinsed to remove any unreacted silver nitrate. Immersing the item then in a solution of photographic "fixer" will halt further development. Since any fixer left in the paper can discolor over time, it is then necessary to wash the item for a substantial amount of time in running water just as a photograph is washed. Wash time can be shortened by the use of a washing aid such as is marketed for similar use for photographic films and papers. All of this means that the item being processed will be wet for a long time in water solutions, which is destructive of many inks. Therefore, before any such chemicals are used, the worker should ascertain first whether the item being processed can withstand the rigors of such processing, and second whether a recording (photographic) of the developed latent print would serve as well as a permanently fixed latent print.

Since the use of a photographic developer will cause the reaction to complete almost immediately, it is suggested that dilute solutions of both the silver nitrate and developer be used. The author has found that solutions of about one-third normal working strength for both solutions is adequate. This allows for somewhat more time for controlling the reactions and is less likely to develop the background to the point that it obscures the latent print.

Other Methods of Developing Latent Prints

There are a great many more methods of development in addition to those that have already been discussed. These methods are suitable, in many instances, for only a particular substrate. Some are quite dangerous; others are interesting but have little or no value to the working latent print examiner.

Heat will develop latent prints on a piece of paper and then setting an ordinary household iron on the paper. If there is a sufficient oily content to the latent prints they will char or scorch before the paper and become quite visible. This is certainly not a practical laboratory development technique.

Heat can be a practical method of developing latent prints but is useful in very few instances. If latent prints on surface are very dry and will not develop with ordinary powder techniques, it is possible to develop them by holding them over the flame of a substance that also produces a dense smoke. The heat of the flame is will soften the latent print residue so that the smoke or soot can adhere to it (Figure 4.18). The item is then very gently brushed or is held under gently running water to reveal the latent prints. Camphor, tarry pine chips, or even plastic will burn to produce a dense black smoke; magnesium can be burned to produce a dense white smoke.

Figure 4.18 Developing latent prints by "smoking".

Benzedine, leuco-malachite green (Olsen, 1978), and ortho-tolidene (Nariyuki et al., 1971) are all blood reagents that have been used successfully to develop prints made with blood. Each of these is or has been used in general criminalistics work as a presumptive test for blood. If properly applied, they will cause their various color reactions on a latent print made of blood, delineating the ridge structure and making the print visible. The key to the successful use of any of these is to apply it in a quick-drying solution so that the blood is not diffused or washed off the substrate. Blood on very absorbent surfaces such as cloth may be fixed by treating with a solution of 70% ethanol in water to prevent the blood from migrating when the reagent is applied (Olsen, 1978).

A solution used in the author's laboratory consists of 0.5 g ortho-tolidene and 0.1 g sodium perborate shaken until dissolved in 10 ml ethanol and 5 ml glacial acetic acid. This is then diluted in 50 ml freon to yield the working solution, which is applied with a sprayer capable of delivering a very fine mist. The item being treated should not be wetted by the spray; two or three applications is usually adequate to turn the blood (if any) a very dark blue. Such prints should be photographed since they are transient. Any blood reagent should be used only with appropriate precautionary measures such as gloves, particle masks, and fume hoods: most are carcinogenic.

Although these reagents used as presumptive tests for blood are very sensitive, it may be preferable simply to use ninhydrin. While less blood-sensitive, ninhydrin does develop it and will also develop other parts of a print not composed of blood, which may result in a more complete print.

Latent prints on glass with an oily or waxy content can be developed by exposing the glass to the fumes of hydrofluoric acid. The oily or waxy content of the latent print acts as a resist, preventing the fumes from etching the glass protected by the deposit. Thus the unprotected glass is etched by the acid whereas that protected by the latent print ridges remains clear. Although this method is certainly workable, there is little question that such a latent print could be developed by other less dangerous techniques.

Latent print deposits acting as a resist is also the mechanism that allows latent prints to be "developed" on items such as brass cartridge cases when exposed to the fumes of nitric acid. Nitric acid is a vigorous oxidizing reagent and should only be used with appropriate precautions. Here again, however, it can be expected that if there is a sufficient amount of oily content to the latent print material to allow it to act as a resist, the latent print will develop using other techniques.

Some items that may bear latent prints of interest or importance to an investigation may be exposed to an environment that is ordinarily detrimental to the common processing techniques. The salts upon which silver nitrate depends for success and the amino acids that are developed by ninhydrin are water soluble. It can be expected, therefore, that items which would otherwise be appropriate for processing with these chemicals but which have been immersed in water would require some processing technique that develops a deposit that is not water soluble, such as sebum or oil. Biological stains have been shown to work in these situations.

Sudan Black-B has been used to develop latent prints on paper items that have been immersed in water for as long as ten days (Mitsui et al., 1980). If the item to be processed is wet when received, it should be allowed to dry. The solution is prepared by mixing 25 mg Sudan Black-B with 5 ml ethylene glycol and adding 10 ml ethanol and 5 ml water. The item is immersed, agitated for a few seconds, removed, blotted to eliminate excess solution, and dried with forced hot air. Latent prints that develop are dark blue.

Also a possibility for use on paper items that have been wet is the use of magnetic or ferrous powder. Because the non-water-soluble component being sought is the oil or waxy component of the latent print, if there is any remaining sufficiently near the surface of the paper, it may develop with this technique. Caution should be exercised since immersion in water will cause the surface of many paper items to become quite loose; the resultant texture of the surface may be sufficient to capture the particles of powder, which would obscure any developed latent print.

Most chemical development techniques produce a dark-colored print; therefore, very dark-colored objects are not suitable for chemicals such as silver nitrate or ninhydrin. Calcium sulfide (1% in water) can be used to develop a light-colored print (Figure 4.19). The item is immersed in the solution and gently agitated. The development must be watched carefully and the item removed before the calcium sulfide covers the surface. After removal the item is allowed to dry without heat. Latent prints so developed may be quite faint.

Potentially more useful is the use of a fluorescent dye, Mikephor BS (Arima, 1981), to develop latent prints on dark surfaces. The dye is mixed to a 1% solution in water and ammonia added to bring the solution to a pH between 7 and 8. The item is immersed for a few minutes and then rinsed and dried. Latent prints fluoresce under long-wave UV.

The same dye is recommended for use on tape where other development techniques, such as powder, cannot be used due to the presence of adhesive. Victoria Blue BOH and Crystal Violet mixed to

Figure 4.19 Latent print developed with calcium sulfide on black paper.

0.1% and brought to pH 7–8 are recommended by the same authors for use on tapes; these produce a visible latent print (Arima, 1981). Although certainly not useful in a great many cases, the ability to develop latent prints on such surfaces can be critical in some situations.

Some of the components of latent print material have a natural luminescence; that is, when illuminated by light of a certain wavelength their energy state is raised and then stablized by the emission of energy at a different wavelength. That biological materials luminesce or fluoresce has been known for some time, but the application of this to latent prints was first reported in a paper in 1977 (Dalrymple et al., 1977). As in so many cases, exploration of this subject came about because of some problems occurring while working on a dissimilar project. The use of the inherent luminescence of latent print material involves the use of a laser.

The instrument commonly used is an argon-ion continuous wave laser. The laser output is a blue–green light; the latent prints luminesce yellow green. For use the beam must be expanded, which is accomplished by placing a diverging lens in the output beam of the laser. The object being examined is placed in the expanded beam and viewed through filters that exclude the blue–green laser light and allow the yellow–green luminescence to pass through. Any latent prints so visualized must be photographed with the same type of filter (Figure 4.20).

Not all latent prints luminesce under laser light; most of those that do, at least with current technology, will also develop satisfactorily with ordinary physical or chemical techniques. Work does continue in this field with investigations of the use of dyes to enhance the luminescence of the latent print material and with modification of the laser wavelength to cause different components of the latent print material to luminesce. However, although a useful, viable technique, the use of lasers is presently limited by the cost of the devices and the fact that they are probably the least portable of all processing techniques.

A potential application of lasers would solve one of the most difficult questions that can be posed to a latent print examiner. The age of a latent print—when it may have been placed on an object—is often asked but seldom answered. At the present time there is no accurate way to determine the age of a latent print by an examination of the print itself. Investigations seem to indicate, however, that as the luminescing components of latent print material age, their emission spectra also change (Duff and Menzel, 1977). It may be that if the use of laser technology for the detection of latent prints achieves its potential, the latent print examiner may thus be able to answer questions regarding the age of a latent print.

Figure 4.20 Latent print "developed" by laser. *(Courtesy of Dr. E.R. Menzel, Texas Tech.)*

It is possible to develop latent prints by a great many techniques that are not mentioned here. Chlorine and bromine vapors, ruthenium dioxide, osmium tetroxide, vacuum metal deposition, transference to specially treated photographic paper, and even the use of radioactive sulpher oxide are all viable techniques: A review of the literature will provide the reader with more information regarding these than is the intention of this work. The purpose of the foregoing is simply to provide an understanding of the complexity of what is being sought (i.e., the latent print) and, hopefully, to engender a willingness to consider that complexity when approaching the task.

Determining the Age of an Evidence Print

As mentioned above, latent print examiners seldom consider the age of prints. The reason for this is quite simple. Evidence prints can be composed of almost any material. The effects of time and environment on these components, although perhaps determinable by sophisticated laboratory techniques, are generally unknown to the average latent print examiner. Also, seldom does the examiner know just what it was that composed the latent print before it was developed: this may be known in the case of prints developed with silver nitrate (salt) or ninhydrin (amino acids), or where the print was made in some recognizable substance such as blood or motor oil; but even if the examiner were able to assay the components of the amino acids, for instance, and determine how much degradation had occurred and the cause of the degradation, it would still be unknown if the material came from the donor of the print or if it got on the donor's hand by contact with another person or some object.

That a latent print develops strongly and quickly does not provide much of a clue to its age since many substances that could cause the print may have sufficient viscosity to remain in one place for long periods of time and do not necessarily dry out even in harsh environments. Prints deposited on porous surfaces may not migrate, or the primary constituent may evaporate, leaving the component being sought (such as salt) dry and trapped in place. Certainly the most accurate determination that can be made with regard to age would be to determine the earliest point in time that the object could have been touched by the individual concerned and then adopt that as the maximum possible age of the print.

If a latent print is developed on a window and it is known that the window had been thoroughly washed 2 months prior to developing the latent print, then, since it is unlikely that a latent print that would develop with powder would survive a thorough washing, its maximum age is 2 months. If a latent print of an individual is found on a piece of paper belonging to the victim of a crime, and that piece of paper had been purchased in packaged condition and opened only 2 days prior to the offense, then the print is probably not more than 2 days old, unless the individual of concern could have handled the paper before it was packaged. Here, the age of the print is not determined from an examination of the print itself, but by considering the circumstances surrounding the object upon which it was found.

Generally speaking, latents prints are affected by their environment. Unless composed of some extraordinarily durable substance they can be expected to dry, harden by evaporation, or diffuse through the substrate unless maintained in a particularily suitable environment. Logically, one would not expect a latent print to improve with time; possibly it will not degrade but likely lose its ability to capture powder, or the salts or amino acids diffuse through the substrate due to high humidity. For an examiner to conclude that a particular print is "old" because little powder adheres or because the print has diffused through the substrate would be to ignore the fact that many latent prints that are quite new have those characteristics.

On the other hand, it may be possible for the experienced latent print examiner to proffer an opinion regarding the maximum age of a latent print if the circumstances are well defined. For example, a latent print found on the exterior of a window is known to have been exposed to periods of sunshine, blowing wind and dust, and rain. In spite of the adverse conditions the latent print shows excellent detail of ridge and even pore structure and powder adheres readily. It would be expected under the defined conditions that the perspiration component of the print, if any, would have been evaporated by the sun or washed away by the rain. The oily component of a print may survive the sun and rain for a substantial period of time but would also be expected to collect dust just as it develops with powder. Also the warming effect of the sun might be expected, over time, to warm the oily component so that is might flow to obscure the edge and pore structure of the print.

Considering these things, the examiner would be faced with deciding how long a latent print could last under such circumstances and still retain the qualities seen in print being examined. Any determination must be a subjective evaluation of what is objectively considered; even then it must be offered only as an estimation based upon the examiner's experience and not excluding other interpretations.

Photography of Prints and Impressions

5

Photography is as important and useful in the field of friction skin comparison and identification as it is in other aspects of the forensic sciences. The purpose of photography in this field is twofold: to record what is seen accurately and permanently for future reference and/or to enhance the appearance of evidence.

Many types of evidence are impermanent, or must be removed from the object that bears them in order to be examined; photographs can permanently record the location and appearance of such evidence. Often the actual collection of an item of evidence may be impractical or impossible because of its size or location; photography must then be employed if an examination and comparison are to be done at all. Photography is also often necessary, regardless of the quality of the evidence print, in order to prepare displays to illustrate the results of comparisons and identifications for court proceedings or other purposes. Finally, when evidence is obscured by its surroundings, or the nature of the evidence itself prevents its visualization by normal techniques, it *may* be possible to utilize the spectral sensitivities and capabilities of various photographic media to advantage.

Photography is not a panacea. While it may be theoretically possible to photograph anything which can be seen and much of what cannot be seen, as a practical matter the use of photography suffers from a number of limiting factors. Two of these are the skill and knowledge of the photographer and the resources available; but even a well equipped and thoroughly knowledgeable photographer will at times find that the product of his or her labor falls short of the anticipated result. That this is so is usually related to the fact that the best camera and most carefully selected film do not equate to the combination of eye and brain.

Whether color or black-and-white, even the best film does not respond to the light spectrum in a manner equivalent to the eye. While this can be, and often is, used to some advantage, it is also a factor which can prevent the production of a photograph that records the evidence as well as it could be seen. Also, the camera "sees" the subject from a single, fixed viewpoint, whereas the eye is constantly moving, adjusting for imperfections, changing its viewpoint, and compensating for differences in lighting and contrast. Thus, although the camera may provide an accurate literal reproduction, it cannot interpret or make allowances for imperfections in the subject as does the human observer.

Photography is an indispensible tool that, when applied intelligently, can be of significant value and improve the effectiveness of the examiner and the usefulness of evidence. It is not, however, necessary for the worker to be expert in the field of photography: equipment and available materials should be familiar, as should how they are best utilized to record evidence prints.

For the most part, the photography of latent prints is a relatively straightforward process. However, many prints are quite faint, some can only be visualized by the difference in reflectivity between the print and the substrate, and some may be obscured by similar-colored backgrounds. In these situations it may be necessary to photograph the print before it can be compared.

The Camera

The camera used to photograph evidence prints does not need to be specialized or even very sophisticated. The primary requirement here is that the camera should be capable of focusing at relatively close distances so that the resulting negative will have a sufficiently large image of the print to retain clarity in the detail of the print when it is enlarged. The size of the negative produced by the camera should, therefore, also be of adequate size to allow the normally expected subject or size of print to be photographed at a reasonably low reduction ratio.

It is possible to purchase cameras designed specifically for the purpose of photographing evidence prints. These use larger-format film—usually 2¼ × 3¼-in. or 4 × 5-in. sheet film—so that negative size is adequate to photograph most evidence prints life size (reduction ratio of 1:1). In fact, these cameras have a reduction ratio that is usually fixed at 1:1 (fixed focus). They also may have built-in or fixed light sources and, with practice, will produce good photographs of most evidence prints.

Ordinary 35-mm camera equipment can be used quite effectively although it would not be possible to photograph a complete palm print at even near life size due to the small (1 × 1½-in.) negative. If care is taken with regard to proper focus and selection of film, with reductions of 1:5 (one-fifth life size) even a large print can be photographed with this film format without noticeable loss of clarity.

Large format (4 × 5-in.) general purpose cameras can be used very effectively in latent print work. The large negative is adequate for reproducing most evidence prints at life size and the usual bellows can allow even larger than life reproduction with short focal length lenses.

Through-the-lens [or single-lens-reflex (SLR)] viewing is most helpful for circumstances requiring critical lighting and is common on 35-mm, and 4 × 5-in., or view camera equipment. The ability to see the subject from the perspective of the shooting lens is at times critical to successfully photographing a subject and assessing the effect of a lighting method.

Ideally the worker will have a selection of equipment for different circumstances: some may need to be conveniently portable for scene work or for use on large bulky objects at the work place or laboratory; other equipment may be fixed to a stand with built-in light, ready for convenient use. Figures 5.1–5.3 show some photographic equipment that is suitable for evidence print work.

Figure 5.1 35-mm camera on a stand to allow fixed focus and reproduction ratio.

Figure 5.2 View camera (4 × 5 in. film size) with an attachment on the lens which allows fixed focus and reproduction ratio.

Figure 5.3 A common type of copy camera with fixed lights and a light table.

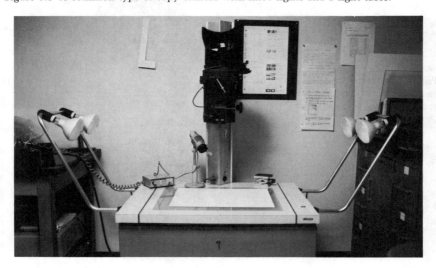

Film

There are many types of film available, most of which are suitable for photographing evidence prints under the right circumstances. Ordinary or "color blind" films are sensitive to only blue light; orthochromatic films are sensitive to all but red light; and panchromatic films are sensitive to all colors of the spectrum. Although a film may be sensitive to a certain portion of the spectrum, its degree of sensitivity is not distributed evenly over that portion: some emulsions have more relative sensitivity to green than to blue, for instance. Even apparently equivalent films of different manufacturers can differ in this respect. Color film is also useful and may, in some circumstances, have some advantage over the monochromatic (black and white) films. Monochromatic and color films also have varying contrast and grain characteristics which can be considered in selecting a film for general use or for a particular task.

For most work a fine-grain, continuous-tone panchromatic film can be used. Of course, the greater the anticipated enlargement (reproduction ratio) of the negative, the more important become the grain characteristics of the film. At small ratios near 1:1 this is seldom a problem. One of the advantages of using a panchromatic film is that it allows the worker to use filtration to enhance or reduce the recording of a particular color.

High-contrast (as opposed to continuous-tone) films can be very effective if the subject is already of high contrast, and can produce beautifully crisp photographs of evidence prints. The characteristics of this type of film are such that exposure is usually somewhat more critical than it is for continuous-tone film. As an example, lithographic materials are high-contrast materials which produce only maximum and minimum density in the negative with no gray tones. If the print being photographed is of varying tonal value, this high-contrast material would not be suitable: some very important areas of the print may fall below the threshold for exposure of the negative and not record at all, going to full black in the resulting photograph; other areas may be lighter and remain completely white in the photograph. If a high-contrast rendering is required of a subject that is not inherently contrasty, it would be well to experiment with raising the contrast of continuous-tone materials by underexposure and overdevelopment of the negative material, or to use continuous-tone negative material and very high-contrast paper for the final photography.

Figure 5.4 illustrates the effect of high-contrast film on a continuous-tone subject. When the latent print was developed with ninhydrin on white paper, there was a small amount of background reac-

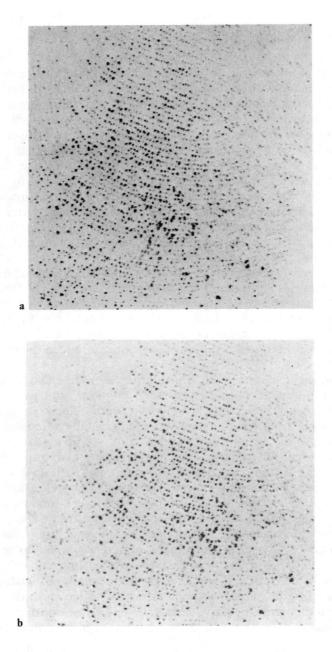

Figure 5.4 Latent print photographed under different conditions. (See text.)

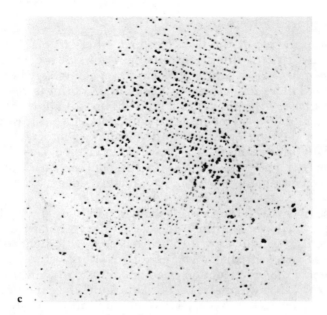

c

Figure 5.4 *(continued)*

tion; it thus appeared as a reddish-purple print against a faintly reddish-purple background. The print was somewhat spotty with some areas showing only very faint connections between the dots. Photographed with a continuous-tone panchromatic film and normal exposure and development produced a literal recording of what was seen [Figure 5.4a]. Photography with the same film, but underexposed by a factor of 4 (two *f*-stops) and developed for twice the normal development time, produced a photograph that shows the ridges with approximately the same density as in the "normal" rendition, but the background appears substantially lighter [Figure 5.4b]. Photographed with negative material designed for high-contrast work, the latent print is recorded as very black against a nicely white background, but the dots appear unconnected and much of the very faint detail is lost [Figure 5.4c].

It should be noted that latent prints developed with black powder and preserved with tape on a white card are, in fact, very high contrast and may appear gray for the same reason the half-tone reproductions in this book appear to have gray in them even though composed of black ink. The greater the concentration of black particles the darker the print will appear.

Use of Colored Filters

The basic principle of the use of colored filters in black and white photography is that a filter transmits light of its own color. A yellow filter transmits yellow light and blocks other colors; a red filter transmits red and blocks other colors. Therefore if a print is developed on a green surface with ninhydrin, a green filter will allow the green of the substrate to expose the negative while blocking, at least partially, the color of the developed print. The resultant photograph will then show a dark print against a relatively lighter colored background. The filter does not effect any change in the contrast characteristics or spectral sensitivity of the film, but merely affects what the film "sees."

Because of the way filters work they are rarely used with blue-sensitive or orthochromatic films: the use of a red filter with an orthochromatic film would allow it to be exposed only to light to which it has little, if any, sensitivity. The use of any other primary color filter causes such a drastic reduction of colors of light to which it is sensitive that the exposure time would become quite long and impractical.

Filters can be used to cause panchromatic films to mimic the effect of ordinary and orthochromatic films by selecting a filter that blocks the unwanted portion of the spectrum. Panchromatic film can yield results similar to orthochromatic film if a green filter is used; the effect is only an approximation, however, and is dependent upon the precise sensitivities of the particular film.

One factor affecting the use of filters is the spectrum emitted by the light source used to expose the film. For instance, the use of blue filters with tungsten illumination is generally inappropriate because such lights are quite deficient in blue light and the filter blocks too much of the rest of the spectrum to allow adequate exposure of the film.

The use of filters can be of great help to the worker if either the developed print or the substrate or both are other than black, white, or gray. To lighten a color, a filter is selected that most closely approximates that color; to darken a color, a filter of a complementary color should be selected (Figure 5.5). If the subject is of the same or a very similar color to the background, as sometimes happens with very faint prints where the color of the background shows through the print, it may be difficult or even impossible to separate the subject from the background photographically by the use of filters.

Lighting

Most evidence prints can be effectively photographed in normal room light or, if necessary, by daylight even if the materials must be taken outdoors. However, it is sometimes necessary to exercise some con-

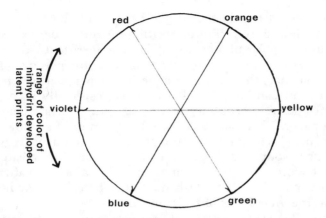

Figure 5.5 Color wheel. To lighten a color, use a filter or similar color. To darken a color, use a filter color opposite it on the circle.

trol over the amount, direction, color, and type of light in order to photograph an evidence print.

To achieve the greatest possible latitude and usefulness of film and filters, light that is rich in all colors of the spectrum is necessary. Such light can be provided by daylight (which is not always available) or, more consistently, with electronic flash. Fortunately, few evidence prints require extreme control of color temperature; continuously burning lamps such as tungsten photoflood or even ordinary light bulbs are therefore quite adequate.

To control the amount and direction of light, reflectors and diffusers are quite useful. It is not necessary for the worker to have a great amount of lighting equipment: much can often be accomplished with a little equipment and a judicious application of imagination.

For high-contrast or continuous-tone black and white subjects, a simple camera setup with the normally used film is easily arranged. With the camera at a reasonable distance with an appropriate reduction ratio and some means of providing relatively even lighting over the subject, a good quality photograph should be the result. Even a single light can produce good results, although two lights at 45° angles to the subject (one on either side) is minimal if truly even lighting is desired. With a single light source, the most even lighting is achieved with the light at a very high angle, or by placing a reflector on the opposite side of the subject from the light. If the light is near vertical and the subject is shiny, the viewfinder or ground glass of the view camera should be carefully checked for "hot spots," which are actually reflections of the light source itself. If the light to be used is an electronic flash unit, a continuously burning light in the anticipated positions of the flash unit can be used to check for hot spots, moving the flash unit back into position for the actual exposure.

Many items to be photographed have a texture to their surface which can be detrimental to obtaining a useful photograph of the print. For instance, the texture of a piece of paper bearing a ninhydrin developed print can be quite objectionable, especially if the print is quite faint and it is necessary to increase the contrast between the print and paper. This occurs because of the minute shadows cast by the paper fibers, which obscure the print. This can happen even with multiple light sources although the effect is certainly greater with a single light source. The texture of other surfaces can also affect a photograph, such as wood and brushed metal. The effect may not be noticeable in the viewfinder of the camera.

When the texture is directional, as on wood or brushed metal, the orientation of the texture on axis with the direction of the light may completely overcome any potential problems. If the texture is random as occurs with paper, diffuse lighting can minimize or eradicate the problem, illuminating the subject from all directions so that the areas shadowed with light from one direction are lit from another.

A very simple diffuse lighting arrangement can be made by using a piece of white translucent paper rolled into an open-top cone. This can be placed over the area of the print and lit from the outside while the camera photographs the print through the top (Figure 5.6). A more efficient technique suitable for small objects is easily set up with a light table or box and a large reflector from a portable light. The item being photographed is placed on an opaque background, to prevent light transmission through and refraction around the item. The reflec-

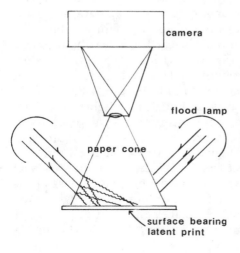

Figure 5.6 Diffuse lighting using a paper cone.

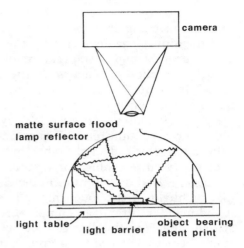

Figure 5.7 Diffuse lighting using a reflector and light table.

tor is placed over it, and the camera is aimed through the hole at the top of the reflector (Figure 5.7). The effect is very diffused light that removes virtually all texture from the subject.

The effect of such diffusion lighting techniques can be seen in Figure 5.8. Figure 5.8a shows a ninhydrin-developed latent print on a piece of rough paper toweling. Although visible, the print is not

Figure 5.8 Ninhydrin-developed latent print photographed **a.** with "ordinary" even lighting and **b.** with lighting as in Figure 5.7.

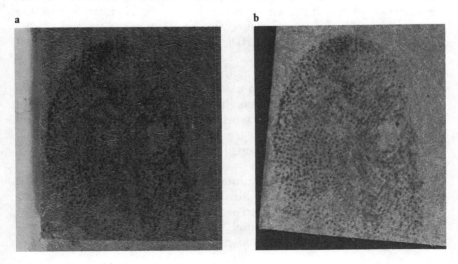

shown as it could be seen with the unaided eye—due, perhaps, to the camera not being able to "see" around the minute paper fibers, and also to minute shadows cast by the lighting arrangement (the standard four-light copy arrangement of Figure 5.3). Figure 5.8b is the same print photographed with the reflector diffusion arrangement shown in Figure 5.7. Here the texture of the paper is virtually eliminated and the print is recorded about as well as could be seen.

Figure 5.9 shows a latent print developed with black powder on a rough piece of aluminum. Figure 5.9a was made with diffuse light using a reflector and a light table. In figure 5.9b, while the latent print is certainly quite visible, the texture of the aluminum surface is very prominent. Had the latent print developed with less density, the specular highlight of the rough metallic surface may have overwhelmed it and made it difficult to compare. For this photograph the light was at right angles to the direction of the striae. In Figure 5.9c, the same single light was placed to illuminate the surface along the axis of the striae. Here the print appears to have ridges that are more complete than when cross-lit and the photograph is a much better rendition of the print than in Figure 5.9b. The general gray tone of the background is caused by powder being trapped by the texture of the surface.

Single light sources, well controlled, can be very effective in allowing developed and undeveloped-but-visible prints to be photographed. This is especially effective when the print is on a highly reflective surface such as a piece of glass, polished metal, or some plastic surfaces, and works by taking advantage of the difference in the reflective properties of the print and the substrate.

One technique involves using a point light source at a fairly low angle to the surface with the camera directly above the print. The light striking the polished surface will reflect off it at the same low angle, whereas the light striking the less smooth substance of the print will be reflected in many directions with some of the light being recorded by the film (Figure 5.10). The result is a photograph that shows a white print on a black background. The original color or tonal value of either the print or the substrate is of no consequence and even a print developed with black powder on a mirror will record as light against dark. Of course it is necessary for ambient light to be dim or nonexistent if the worker is to exercise adequate control over the lighting of the subject for this to work as well as it might. Figure 5.11 shows an undeveloped latent print on a mirror photographed in this manner.

Axis lighting is another technique that makes use of a directional point light source, directed to the subject along the same axis as the lends of the camera. For this to work properly the subject must be flat and parallel to the film plane. This lighting technique is accomplished by placing a half-silvered mirror or even a piece of ordinary

Figure 5.9 Latent print developed with black powder on rough aluminum **a.** photographed as in Figure 5.7; **b.** photographed with a single light at 45°, at right angles to the axis of the striae. **c.** Same as (**b**) but with the light parallel to the direction of the striae.

glass below the lens at 45° to the lens axis. The light source is placed horizontally and aimed to strike the mirror or glass at a point directly below the lens. The light is reflected straight down to the subject and the camera is able to photograph the result through the transparent mirror or glass. The light striking the smooth surface will be reflected straight up through the glass or mirror to the camera, whereas that

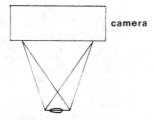

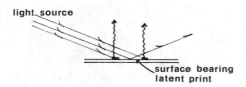

Figure 5.10 Low-angle "oblique" lighting.

Figure 5.11 Undeveloped latent print on a mirror photographed as in Figure 5.10.

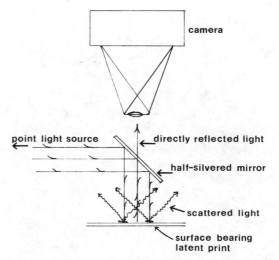

Figure 5.12 Axis lighting.

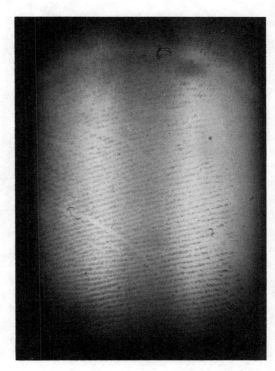

Figure 5.13 Undeveloped latent print on a mirror, photographed as in Figure 5.11.

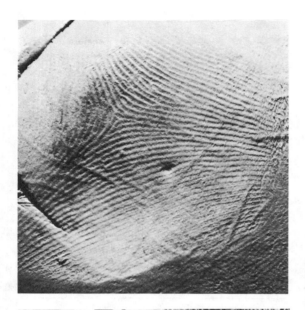

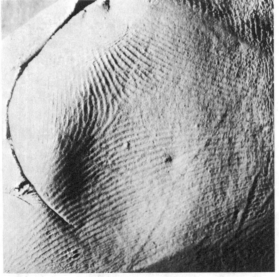

Figure 5.14 Plastic impression photographed **a.** with the light from the top of the picture and **b.** with the light from the left of the picture. Both photographed as in Figure 5.10.

which strikes the less smooth substance of the print will be scattered with relatively less being recorded by the film (Figure 5.12). The result is a dark print on a light background in the final photograph. Ambient light must, of course, be controlled. Figure 5.13 is a photograph of the same print as in Figure 5.11. It should be noted that the banded gray area in which the print appears is actually a reflection of the light source, which was, in this instance, a small two-bulb fluorescent unit. With this type of lighting success is limited by the reflective characteristics of the substrate bearing the print, the size of the print, and the size of the spot of light reflected to the surface by the reflector. The larger the print to be photographed, the larger the spot of light must be in order to encompass the entire print. Substrates more suitable for this lighting technique than mirrors of highly polished metals would be, simply, smooth shiny surfaces such as many plastics or blued weapons such as revolvers. This technique, like that of oblique lighting, is limited to flat or nearly flat substrates.

Low-angle, oblique light from a point light source is also used to photograph plastic impressions. In this case the depressed areas are shadowed and only the higher areas are lit. The depressed areas that are parallel to the direction of the light will not be shadowed; therefore it may be necessary to take more than one photograph if a single photograph of the subject print in any one orientation to the light will not record a significant amount of the print. If more than one photograph is necessary, it may be possible to subsequently combine a number of photographs to make the print "whole" for comparison purposes. If this is to be done, the relationship between the camera and subject should not be changed between photographs, only the light being moved (Figure 5.14).

Highly reflective surfaces reflect their environment, and it may be necessary to reduce unwanted reflections that can, at times, include the camera or even the worker. Tent lighting techniques are very effective at eliminating environmental reflections but may limit the

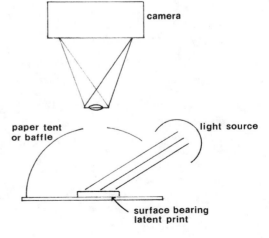

Figure 5.15 Partial tent or baffle to exclude environmental reflections.

paper tent or baffle

camera

light source

surface bearing latent print

control the worker desires over the amount of light and certainly remove control of the direction of the light. A partial tent or even a
baffle of cardboard, usually white, fitted over the lens of the camera
will still allow the worker adequate control over the lighting while
the film "sees" only the subject against the reflection of the selected
baffle or partial tent (Figure 5.15). This can be useful when the print
is on a surface which is not flat and therefore is not suitable for
oblique or axis illumination.

The Basis of the Comparison 6

Class Characteristics

Class characteristics of friction ridge prints are those characteristics that can be possessed by more than one print. Even though a class characteristic may be possessed by millions of prints, it can still be of value to the individualization or identification process. This is so because such characteristics reduce the population of prints that must be effectively eliminated before a condition of identity or common source for two prints can be stated with certainty.

One of the precepts which workers in the field of friction ridge comparison hold is that to identify a print conclusively is to exclude every other piece or portion of friction skin that has ever existed. Therefore, if a print was made by a particular finger or portion of palm or sole or toe of a particular individual it could not be duplicated by any other segment of friction skin that has ever existed. As a practical matter, however, it is seldom necessary to consider whether the arrangement of the individual characteristics is adequate to achieve this lofty conclusion: the number of potential donors for any particular print is limited by geography and time, and class characteristics of a print serve to reduce the number of potential donors in any given population.

Consider a hypothetical situation with a truly limited population. A poisoning occurs on an ocean liner, the poison being administered with a tea cup that has definitely been washed since leaving port. Developed on the cup is a friction ridge print showing a particular pattern type. If only two individuals in the ship's entourage possess that pattern type, then the number of potential donors has been reduced to two based solely on class characteristics. In practice, the population that is considered is not nearly so limited and may include thousands and even millions of individuals.

A more practical potential use of class characteristics in the individualization of friction ridge prints, which remains only potential for the forseeable future, is their use as an adjunct to the individualization process itself. Consider, for example, an evidence print which contains the minimum number of "individual" characteristics which would allow an average examiner to reach a decision of conclusive identity and which has no significant class characteristics. Figure 6.1 is an example of such a print. Most examiners with whom the author is acquainted would have no qualms about identifying such a print with ten, or even eight characteristics. If such a quantity of "individual" characteristics is adequate to exclude every other section of friction skin except that which made the print, then how much would be necessary if it were known that the print was made by a right index finger? Right index fingers constitute only one-tenth of all fingers and but a small fraction of the friction skin possessed by a nor-

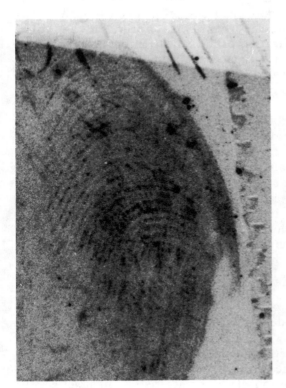

Figure 6.1 Print with minimal "individual" characteristics.

mal individual. What would be necessary number of minutiae if, in addition to the knowledge that the print was made by a particular digit, it was known that the pattern type of the print occurs on only one of ten of that digit? (It should be noted here that the conditions are not cumulative: since almost everyone has a right index finger, knowledge of pattern and digit still only excludes nine-tenths of the population.)

A rhetorical question is to be posed at this point: if ten (or eight or twelve) characteristics are adequate to exclude every individual except the donor, then how many are necessary if the population of potential donors is reduced by a factor of ten? One less individual characteristic? Two less? The question is rhetorical because there is, at this time, no way to define minimum quantitive or qualitative standards for the identification of any print. This is not to imply that class characteristics should be ignored—quite the contrary—but they should be used with caution and circumspection.

The most usual and obvious use of class characteristics is as a means of elimination or exclusion; that is, an evidence print with an obvious whorl pattern could not have been made by a person whose fingers or palms possess no such pattern. When such class characteristics are clear, opinions of conclusive nonidentity can be formed and expressed with a rapidity that sometimes seems to amaze the uninitiated. Often, the available class characteristics will neither clearly include nor exclude a particular finger or palm, but may instead simply limit the amount of work the examiner must do. For example, some prints are of such quality that it is not possible to determine what the class characteristics are, but it is possible to determine what they are not. A print that was obviously made by a palm with a particular orientation that shows a single clear triradius would not have to be compared in all three possible orientations for the triradius. Here, while the population of potential donors is limited only a little, if at all, by the class characteristics, at least the amount of work that must be done is greatly reduced.

The class characteristics of friction ridged skin extend to many factors other than digit or palm (or toe or sole) and definable pattern type. Patterns of the same type, by definition, may appear quite different. Thus it is not necessary to consider only whether a pattern is a loop, for instance, but also the size of the loop, the presence or absence of converging ridges, the degree of the slope of the pattern, and even the amount of curvature that may be present. The examiner may consider all of these things, allowing for distortion, before beginning to look for individual characteristics such as ending ridges and bifurcations. It is unlikely that an obviously well recorded print that shows very narrow, closely spaced ridges would be compared (for individualizing characteristics) to a print with very broad, widely spaced ridges that is also well recorded.

Because of the nature of friction skin, the examiner must exercise caution and not impute a class characteristic to a print without considering whether it actually existed in the skin that made the print, or could have been caused by some imperfection in the recording process. Ridges can be pressed together, stretched apart, twisted, distorted, or overlain by other prints: all of these, and more, can cause a print to look different than if it were well and carefully recorded. Experience with many comparisons will allow the examiner to be better able to consider such factors and their possible effects.

Figure 8.1 (p. 194) shows a latent print that appears to possess certain class characteristics of a particular pattern, distances between deltas and core, angular relationship between landmarks, shape of the circuiting ridges at the center of the pattern, and so on. Close examination of the print, however, shows a "disturbed" area running diagonally across the pattern, which may have been caused by slippage or slight movement of the digit while in light contact with the surface, or even by the surface on which the print was placed. In this case, however, what seem to be at least reasonably good class characteristics of a single print are actually caused by a combination of prints of two different digits belonging to the same individual. This same type of problem can certainly also occur with prints of two different persons, and the examiner should be aware of the possible implications when part of a print seems out of character for other parts.

Studies have shown that the distribution of class characteristics can vary in different populations. Thus, an estimation of the frequency of occurrence of a particular pattern type based upon data from a particular population may be inaccurate if applied to a different group of people. Such a difference may be problematic if the data the examiner uses are obtained from valid sample of population of the geographic region in which the examiner works. An examiner whose work derives from a population of primarily European stock should not, therefore, be too concerned that Koreans exhibit a much greater incidence of whorl patterns. Even if the donor of an evidence print is known to be of a racial or ethnic type with a demonstrable difference in class characteristic distribution, the application of data from a homogeneous data base would not necessarily be unfair to a suspected donor as long as race or ethnic background were not considered to be cumulative with the other data. If such identifying information is known and it is desired to make use of the frequency of occurrence of class characteristics, then an appropriate data base should certainly be used.

Beside the distribution of pattern types, other characteristics have been shown to differ to some degree between population of different racial or ethnic stock (Mukherjee, 1966; Datta, 1966; Cummins and Midlo, 1961). The examiner should not, however, view any data regarding class characteristics as a means of predicting race, ethnic background, or sex no matter how greatly the frequency of distribution of the characteristic may vary from group to group. It is not valid, for instance, to predict that the donor of a particular print is a Korean because the print has a whorl pattern: any pattern type of any size may occur in any population.

It may at times be valid for an examiner to assume that a print was made by a child because of the diminutive size of the print. Likewise, an examiner with sufficient experience may, if circumstances warrant, proffer the opinion that a print could have been or was unlikely to have been made by a female since prints made by females generally exhibit smaller patterns and finer ridges than those of males. However, since such characteristics are by no means exclusive to either sex, such determination should not be presented in a manner that could be construed as conclusive.

The frequency of occurrence of various pattern types has been investigated by many people, beginning with Galton (1892). These studies have been concerned primarily with genetics and inheritance; at least one investigated its use as a means of determining paternity (Holt, 1968). Regarding the use of class characteristics as an adjunct to the individualization of friction skin by individual characteristics, little has been done.

When an individual evidence print or group of such prints is inadequate for identification or exclusion based upon a comparison of the minutiae or ridge characteristics, knowledge of the frequency of occurrence of a particular pattern type, a particular pattern type in a certain finger, or a series of pattern types in a group of fingers may serve to elevate the value of the evidence prints. Just as it is possible to type blood and determine the percentage of the general population that could have bled at a crime scene, so it is possible to determine with a reasonable degree of accuracy the percentage of a population who possess a whorl pattern in the right middle finger, or a whorl pattern in the right thumb and a radial loop in the right index finger. Although such information is certainly insufficient to support a criminal conviction on its own, it can serve as cumulative evidence to include a particular individual as one of a small part of the population who could have been present at the scene of the crime. Such information can also serve to exclude a particular individual, assuming the evidence prints are known to have been made by the one responsible for the crime, just as can blood and hair left at a crime scene.

In the past, frequency of occurrence data were generated from relatively small populations, sometimes comprising as few as a several hundred individuals. Data regarding frequency of occurrence for groups of fingers were generated from bases just as small and were usually concerned with similar digits on opposite hands, as were reported by Cummins and Midlo (1961). Some of the larger studies encompassing thousands of individuals were concerned with pattern intensity as it related to genetic studies. The latent print examiner is not concerned with genetics as a practical matter, and seldom has use for, or interest in, how frequently both index fingers are loops or whorls: rarely will two evidence prints be known to be the index fingers of the same individual.

The latent print examiner is fortunate when able to determine which hand and finger made a particular evidence print; even so, it is seldom that the similar finger of the other hand is also found and can be properly identified as such. The examiner is therefore usually concerned with prints from one hand, singly or as a group. Of interest are the following: How often does a pattern type appear? How often does a particular pattern type appear in a certain finger? How often does a sequence of pattern types appear in a group of prints?

In addressing these questions, the author was fortunate in obtaining data from a very large data base of over 100,000 individuals regarding pattern types and sizes in the various fingers. The author was also fortunate to have the use of a reasonable, though much smaller, data base from which frequency of occurrence of grouping of pattern types could be extracted. Comparison of general pattern frequencies of the larger data base with those of the smaller shows no significant difference, which indicates that the grouping frequencies from the smaller data base are reasonably accurate. Both data bases have about 7% female subjects and 35% Negro.

That frequencies of occurrence can vary is illustrated in Table 6.1,

Table 6.1 Percent Frequency of Occurrence of Pattern Types: Data from Three Sources

Pattern	Source[a]		
	Holt (1968)	Cummins & Midlo (1905)	Cowger (1982)
Whorl	26.1	25.4	30.4
Ulnar loop	63.5	64.0	56.2
Radial loop	5.4	5.7	3.6
Arches	5.0	4.9	9.8

[a]The data presented by Cummins and Midlo were collected by Scotland Yard in 1905. The data from Holt were determined from a "randomly" selected group of 1000, evenly divided by sex.

which compares data from Holt (1968) Cummins and Midlo (1961) with those of the author. Even allowing for some differences in interpretation of pattern types, there is still a substantial difference in the frequencies of occurrence of pattern types. That some of the differences can be attributed to a different racial or ethnic mix in the populations is certain: whereas Holt's population was evenly divided by sex, that of the author has few females. However, adjusting for Holt's much greater female population still leaves a 3% greater incidence of whorl patterns in the author's data. The source of the differences in frequencies may be the difference in sample size or method of selection. (Holt's sample was 1000 "randomly" selected subjects; the author's was essentially an entire file of 135,000 subjects with the only criterion being criminal activity of some sort.)

Table 6.2 is a tabulation of the percent frequency of occurrence of the major pattern types by finger. Here it is easy to see that the different pattern types occur with varying frequencies in the fingers. Because of this uneven distribution, the significance of a particular pattern type in a particular finger can either be of little import or quite significant. For instance, if an evidence print is known to be a left little finger and is an ulnar (left-sloping) loop, the pattern type would not be very discriminating as a class characteristic. If, on the other hand, the print were a radial loop, the class characteristic (pattern type) would be very discriminating, since it would reduce the population of potential donors to about one-fourth of 1% (0.27%) of the total population.

The reader is cautioned to view the data in a general way and apply it conservatively. Although the sample sizes, whether 1000 or over 100,000, may seem large to some, the author believes that even larger samples will be necessary for confidence to be expressed to the 0.001% or even 0.01% level. Because of the size of the data base used

Table 6.2 Percent Frequency of Occurrence of Pattern Types by Finger for 135,000 Subjects

Pattern	Finger									
	1	2	3	4	5	6	7	8	9	10
Plain arch	3.02	8.12	5.37	1.90	1.48	5.21	8.23	6.95	2.54	1.86
Tented arch	0.95	11.29	7.08	3.31	3.87	1.45	11.66	7.06	3.16	3.54
Radial loop	0.65	16.26	1.55	1.25	0.42	0.72	13.25	1.13	0.60	0.27
Ulnar loop	47.06	30.50	66.31	45.50	76.40	55.43	36.06	65.84	57.55	81.63
Whorl	48.32	33.45	19.69	48.05	17.83	37.19	30.80	19.03	36.14	12.70

The data used were provided by the Department of Justice, State of California.

to calculate grouping frequencies, the author did not feel that using class characteristics beyond general pattern type would yield sufficiently large groups to be of significance. For this same reason, groups including plain and tented arches and radial loops in other than index fingers were also not tabulated.

Frequency of occurrence of sizes of pattern in the individual fingers could be determined from the larger data base with some confidence since the numbers of individual "measured" fingers ranged from 129,968 little fingers for each hand to 133,024 left thumbs (Table 6.3). The sizes of the patterns were determined by measuring the distance from the core to delta for loop patterns and from the topographical center of a whorl to the delta on the left for right hands and to the delta on the right for left hands (i.e., the whorls were measured as if they were ulnar loops.)

The unit of measurement used in 0.9 mm, which is approximately two average ridge intervals. The placement of delta and core or whorl center with respect to one another affects the angle at which the measured distance crosses the intervening ridges: the greater the deviation from perpendicular, the fewer ridges will be necessary for each unit of measurement. It should also be noted that ridge counts of males and females tend to differ statistically, with females averaging slightly smaller ridge counts than males.

It is interesting to note that pattern sizes tend to cluster; that is, they are not evenly distributed but tend toward an "average" size. The practical application is that the larger and smaller sizes become statistically significant when they appear in any finger. The largest patterns appear with the least frequency, but it should be pointed out that the larger the pattern, the less likely it is to find both core and delta in an evidence print. Table 6.4 is a tabulation of the mean distance from delta to core (or to topographical center, for whorls) for

Table 6.3 Mean Delta-to-Core Distance[a] by Pattern Type and Finger for 135,000 Subjects

Pattern	Finger									
	1	2	3	4	5	6	7	8	9	10
Radial loop	7.4	7.7	7.2	5.8	5.4	7.0	6.7	6.0	5.7	6.0
Ulnar loop	8.5	6.5	6.9	7.8	7.1	8.0	6.9	7.2	8.2	7.3
Whorl	8.0	4.9	5.8	6.5	5.8	7.6	5.2	6.5	7.0	6.2

The data used were provided by the Department of Justice, State of California.

[a]Unit = 0.9 mm (~2 average ridge intervals).

The units of measure are millimeters. Whorls are measured from delta to the topographical center of the whorl as if they were ulnar loops. There are approximately two ridge counts per 0.9 mm.

Table 6.4 Percent Frequency of Occurrence of Pattern Sizes[a] by Pattern Type for 135,000 Subjects

Pattern	<3 mm, <6 r.c.	3–6 mm, 6–12 r.c.	6–9 mm, 12–18 r.c.	9–12 mm, 18–24 r.c.	12–15 mm, 24–30 r.c.
Radial loop	10.7	43.7	29.7	13.1	2.9
Ulnar loop	5.2	28.4	42.5	21.8	2.1
Whorl	10.7	39.5	40.2	9.0	0.7

[a]Sizes given in millimeters (mm) and ridge counts (r.c.).

135,000 subjects, and illustrates that different pattern types tend to have different average sizes.

Latent print examiners are often faced with evidence prints that comprise a homologous group; that is, a group of individual prints may represent the simultaneous printing of more than one finger of the same hand. By the sequence and heights of the individual prints it is quite possible to determine the finger responsible for each print and, even if the individual fingers are not capable of being individualized, or even if the entire group lacks sufficient detail for individualization, the group is not necessarily valueless.

As has been done with individual digits, combinations of pattern types can be tabulated to determine their frequency of occurrence (Table 6.5). If there were no relationship between the occurrence of pattern types on various fingers, it would be a simple matter to calculate the probability of occurrence for the combination of pattern types and even pattern sizes. That there is a relationship between fingers is without question. The effect is that the appearance of a particular pattern type on one finger increases the probability of occurrence of a similar type on another finger with a concomitant reduction of the probability of occurrence of a dissimilar pattern type. As an example, if the pattern types of the individuals were totally independent, then simple multiplication of the percent frequency of occurrence for whorls would indicate that all ten fingers being whorls would occur in but 0.00026% of all fingerprint cards. This event occurs, however, at a rate of approximately 3%. Therefore, of interest to the worker is how frequently the various combinations of pattern do appear.

In the author's experience, certain grouping of fingers tend to appear in evidence prints. These may include two, three, or four fingers of a single hand, and only occasionally include the little fingers. Complete groups may have one or more missing or undecipherable fingerprints. For these reasons the tables were constructed in the manner

Table 6.5 Percent Frequency of Occurrence of Pattern Types[a] in Combinations of Fingers

Comb. No.	1	2	3	4	5	6	7	8	9	10	Actual % Freq. of Occur.	Calc. % Freq. of Occur.
1	U	U									20.7	16.4
2	U		U								38.7	1.2
3	U			U							30.1	21.4
4		U	U								29.2	20.2
5		U		U							19.6	13.9
6			U	U							41.7	30.2
7						U	U				26.1	20.0
8						U		U			46.3	36.5
9						U			U		41.3	31.9
10							U	U			31.5	23.7
11							U		U		25.3	20.7
12								U	U		49.5	37.9
13	W	W									23.9	16.2
14	W		W								12.9	9.5
15	W			W							30.9	23.2
16		W	W								13.4	6.6
17		W		W							25.7	16.1
18			W	W							16.3	9.5
19						W	W				17.8	11.4
20						W		W			11.5	7.1
21						W			W		19.1	13.4
22							W	W			13.1	5.9
23							W		W		18.9	11.1
24								W	W		13.6	6.9
25	U	R									10.5	7.6
26		R	U								15.5	10.8
27		R		U							11.9	7.4
28						U	R				11.5	7.3
29							R	U			13.9	8.7

(continued)

Table 6.5 *(continued)*

Comb. No.	|1	2	3	4	5	6	7	8	9	10	Actual % Freq. of Occur.	Calc. % Freq. of Occur.
30							R		U		13.3	7.6
31	U	W									10.4	15.7
32	W	U									11.2	14.7
33	U		W								4.6	9.3
34	W		U								32.3	32.0
35	U			W							17.5	22.6
36	W			U							17.0	22.0
37		U	W								1.9	6.0
38		W	U								20.4	22.2
39		U		W							11.9	14.7
40		W		U							9.0	15.2
41			U	W							30.5	31.9
42			W	U							1.2	9.0
43						U	W				12.3	17.1
44						W	U				10.4	13.4
45						U		W			5.1	10.5
46						W		U			22.3	24.5
47						U			W		17.0	20.0
48						W			U		16.9	21.4
49							U	W			3.0	6.9
50							W	U			18.0	20.3
51							U		W		11.8	13.0
52							W		U		12.3	17.7
53								U	W		21.5	23.8
54								W	U		3.4	10.9
55	W	R									9.5	7.9
56		R	W								2.3	3.2
57		R		W							8.7	7.8
58						W	R				6.4	4.9

(continued)

Table 6.5 Percent Frequency of Occurrence of Pattern Types[a] in Combinations of Fingers *(continued)*

Comb. No.	1	2	3	4	5	6	7	8	9	10	Actual % Freq. of Occur.	Calc. % Freq. of Occur.
59							R	W			1.7	2.5
60							R		W		4.5	4.8
61	U	U	U								18.4	9.5
62	U	U	W								0.9	2.8
63	U	W	U								7.1	10.4
64	U	W	W								10.0	9.8
65	W	U	U								1.0	2.9
66	W	U	W								29.9	31.0
67	W	W	U								13.0	10.7
68	W	W	W								10.4	3.2
69						U	U	U			21.8	13.2
70						U	U	W			1.6	3.8
71						U	W	U			9.6	11.2
72						U	W	W			8.6	8.8
73						W	U	U			1.3	2.5
74						W	U	W			2.5	3.2
75						W	W	U			8.2	7.5
76						W	W	W			9.4	2.2
77		U	U	U							18.3	9.2
78		U	U	W							10.1	9.7
79		U	W	U							0.1	2.7
80		U	W	W							7.9	10.1
81		W	U	U							12.7	10.6
82		W	U	W							1.7	2.9
83		W	W	U							0.9	3.0
84		W	W	W							12.5	3.2
85							U	U	U		22.4	13.7
86							U	U	W		8.8	8.6
87							U	W	U		0.8	3.9

(continued)

Table 6.5 *(continued)*

Comb. No.	Finger										Actual % Freq. of Occur.	Calc. % Freq. of Occur.
	1	2	3	4	5	6	7	8	9	10		
88							U	W	W		10.1	11.6
89							W	U	U		8.6	7.3
90							W	U	W		2.3	2.5
91							W	W	U		1.9	3.4
92							W	W	W		10.3	2.1
93	U	R	U								8.0	5.1
94	U	R	W								0.8	1.5
95	W	R	U								7.1	5.2
96	W	R	W								1.5	1.5
97	U	R		U							6.7	3.5
98	U	R		W							3.4	3.7
99	W	R		U							4.7	3.6
100	W	R		W							1.5	3.8
101		R	U	U							9.8	4.9
102		R	U	W							5.7	5.2
103		R	W	U							0.3	1.5
104		R	W	W							2.0	1.5
105						U	R	U			9.1	13.2
106						U	R	W			0.7	3.8
107						W	R	U			4.5	8.8
108						W	R	W			1.0	2.5
109						U	R		U		9.2	11.5
110						U	R		W		2.1	7.5
111						W	R		U		3.8	7.7
112						W	R		W		2.4	4.8
113							R	U	U		10.7	13.7
114							R	U	W		3.0	8.6
115							R	W	U		0.6	3.9
116							R	W	W		1.2	2.5

[a]U, ulnar loop; W, whorl; R, radial loop. Data collected from 1036 fingerprint cards.

in which they appear. Radial loops were considered only in index fingers because of their common occurrence in those digits. Plain and tented arches were not tabulated because their infrequent occurrence, combined with the size of the data base, would have caused an unreliably low response rate; the same holds true for radial loops in other than index fingers.

The data presented include the actual percent frequency of occurrence and the calculated percent frequency of occurrence to indicate the dependency or relationship of the fingers.

Individual Characteristics

The individualizing characteristics of friction skin are those features of the ridges which make it possible to characterize or identify a particular print as having been made by a particular person. Sometimes referred to as "Galton details," minutiae, and even as "points," these characteristics are considered with respect to their location, general appearance, orientation, and interrelationship when comparison is made between two prints.

From a purely technical viewpoint, even the smallest area of friction skin is probably unique. In *Crime Investigation*, Paul Kirk provides the following illustration:

> Two crystals of table salt of dimensions as accurately alike as can be measured, will have the same crystal lattice, the same properties, color, density, chemical reactivity, and so forth. For practical purposes they are absolutely identical, but they will probably never have exactly the same number of crystal ions, and therefore they are not identical in the absolute sense at all. (Kirk, 1974, p. 71)

The illustration is compelling. If two prints being compared were perfectly recorded even though one consisted only of a small section of a single ridge, it would theoretically be possible always to be able to determine whether they share a common source if neither has changed significantly.

Poroscopy and edgeoscopy are examples of attempts to put this into practice. In *poroscopy*, what is compared is the shape and arrangement of the pores of the friction ridges. *Edgeoscopy*, as its name implies, is concerned with the contour or shape of the edges of the ridges. Figure 6.2 shows a print in which the pore shape and arrangement and the ridge contours can be easily seen. There is certainly nothing inherently wrong with the use of either of these types of comparison and, with adequate materials for comparison, the results can be valid. The author is aware of very few cases where such comparisons have been attempted and is not aware of any that have been

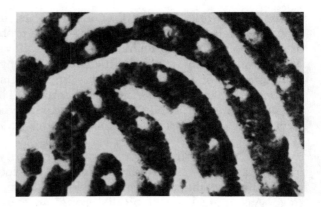

Figure 6.2 Pore shape and arrangement and ridge contours.

adjudicated. The reason for this lack of use of such a logical extension of the theory that nature never repeats itself becomes evident with only a little experience in comparing prints: prints of friction skin are rarely so well recorded in even one print, not to mention both evidence and exemplar prints, that comparison of pores or edges is only rarely practical. Another even more practical consideration is that an evidence print of such minute proportions that poroscopy or edgeoscopy would be necessary would be generally very difficult to compare to all the ridges on the hands of even one potential or suspected donor. If there were a number of suspected donors the task would be formidable indeed. The most practical potential value of the comparison of pores or edge contours would be their use as additional evidence of identity, where the more traditional characteristics are quite limited but the print is otherwise well recorded.

The more traditional characteristics are, of course, the Galton details or minutiae that are features of the friction ridges. The terms used to define and describe these characteristics vary markedly among writers in the field and differ even among examiners depending upon the organization in which they were trained. The Federal Bureau of Investigation, U.S. Department of Justice, generally considers there to be only three types of characteristic (FBI, 1972): the ending ridge, bifurcation, and the dot, all other characteristics being combination of these. This view is specifically supported by at least one other writer (Olsen, 1978). Others have named the combinations of these three basic characteristics and arrived at as many as 12 different types of characteristic (Gupta, 1968). These lengthy lists are generally used in attempts to determine the relative frequency of occurrence of the characteristics so that some objective value or weight can be assigned to them. This is done in order to make the comparison process less subjective.

One such work (Osterburg et al., 1977) is, in the authors' view, especially significant in that it considers the probability of occurrence of groups of individual characteristics as well as single occurrences. The authors of this work defined ten different characteristics and, placing a grid of 1-mm squares over fingerprints, tabulated the characteristics that occurred in each square. They then calculated the negative log probability for the appearance of a particular characteristic or combination of characteristics in a particular square (Table 6.6).

One factor that the authors could not quantify was the appearance of the particular characteristics. Just as the loop pattern can differ greatly in appearance, so can a characteristic as simple as an ending ridge. Assuming little or no distortion, an ending ridge may appear blunt or sharp, or may terminate nearer to the ridge on one side or the other; alternatively, the ridges on either side may flow smoothly together or may pull together sharply before continuing as parallel ridges. However, the effects of pressure, distortion, differences in printing, and irregularities in or on the surface of the substrate will often require the examiner to have to decide whether what is seen is, indeed, the same type of characteristic and the amount of consideration it should be given. Where these types of determination must be made, the judgment of the examiner can be a critical factor in the correctness of the final conclusion. Table 6.7 illustrates some variations of the appearance of the "minimum" characteristics.

Attempts to quantify fingerprint characteristics should neither be taken too literally nor ignored. Even though such efforts have not yet produced a means to define objectively the point at which an identification is proved, they clarify for experienced examiners many factors that were previously known only empirically and give novices information that their predecessors learned only after much experience.

There is a side benefit to be gained from such studies. Galton (1892), after much work, estimated the number of possible configurations of an entire fingerprint to be 6.4×10^9 and the probability of duplication, therefore, to be 1 in 4. Osterburg et al. (1977), using more modern statistical methods, calculate the probability of occurrence of only 12 of the most common characteristics in a particular configuration to be about 10^{-20}. The weights assigned to the characteristics in that work are such that Galton's figures would be reached with but nine such ending ridges, which would be a small part of an entire fingerprint. It is apparent that, as better mathematical models of friction ridge skin are constructed, the stronger and more valid becomes the concept of the individuality of friction skin.

Table 6.6 Frequency of Occurrence of Ridge Characteristics and Assigned Weights[a]

Type of Characteristic	Illustration	Est. of Prob.	Weight[b]
No characteristic		0.7660	0.116
Ending ridge		0.0832	1.08
Fork (bifurcation)		0.0382	1.42
Island ridge or short ridge		0.0177	1.75
Dot		0.0151	1.82
Bridge		0.0122	1.91
Spur		0.0074	2.13
Eye (island)		0.0064	2.19
Double bifurcation		0.0014	2.85
Delta		0.0020	2.70
Trifurcation		0.0006	3.24
Broken ridge		0.0139	1.86
Other multiple occ.		0.0355	1.45

From: *Osterburg et al.* (1977).

[a]The types of characteristic considered by Osterburg et al. (1977) and their frequency of occurrence.
[b]Summing the weights assigned to the characteristics for those found in a print will give the negative log probability of occurrence of that combination of characteristics; i.e., a sum of 18 equals a probability of 10^{-18}, or 0.000,000,000,000,000,001.

Table 6.7 Variations in Appearance of the Minimum Characteristic Form

Bifurcation	Ending Ridge	Dot

Determining Identity

Every friction ridge print either was or was not made by a particular person. This truism would apply even if friction skin was not susceptible to individualization by comparison of class and individual characteristics. There are, unfortunately, two factors which limit the ability of the examiner always to be able to determine whether two prints were made by the same person.

The first limiting factor is the present inability to determine the amount of observable characteristics which must be present in a print for it to be considered unique. Since the inception of the use of friction skin to identify persons, numerous attempts have been made to define a minimum number of characteristics (ending ridges, bifurcations, etc.) that must match with respect to type, location, orientation, and interrelationship in order to consider two prints as proven to have been made by the same person; work toward this end continues on many fronts. Until such an objective standard is developed, an "identification" is made when, *in the judgment of the examiner,* the degree of similarity between two prints is sufficient to warrant that conclusion. T. Dickerson Cooke, one of the most respected workers in the field once wrote:

> Pronouncing that two friction skin impressions, whether from fingers, palms, toes or soles, were or were not made by the same area of friction

skin is an art, not an exact science. It is entirely a matter of judgment based on training and experience. (Cooke, 1973)

No less an authority than the International Association for Identification (1973), found after a three year study, that "no valid basis exists at this time for requiring that a pre-determined minimum number of friction ridge characteristics must be present in two impressions in order to establish a positive identification." The U.S. Federal Bureau of Investigation (1973), in its book *"The Science of Fingerprints,"* states only that "twelve characteristics are ample to illustrate an identification, but it is neither claimed nor implied that this number is required."

Many governments have established minimum quantitative standards for proof of identity; in some areas standards are adhered to that are more traditional than required. Often, standards are set by the agency for which an examiner works (or even by the examiner who desires a personal benchmark) in an attempt to ensure uniformity and prevent error. Minimum standards range from the 16 required at Scotland Yard and 17 in France to, reportedly, as few as three (Mehta, 1963).

A review of literature in the forensic sciences will disclose a range of standards that may be baffling to the student. Kirk (1973) states that "(In the United States) it is customary to find seven or eight points of identity before an identical source can be claimed." Moenssens (1969) states unequivocally that "no less than eight characteristic points" must be found. "The minimum number of ridge characteristics necessary for positive identification is therefore fixed at 11" was the conclusion of Gupta (1968). With such a bewildering array of standards, how is the novice to know when the result of a particular comparison is adequate to support an identification? Unfortunately there is even more to the task of comparison than standards for the number of necessary characteristics would suggest.

An examiner may easily keep tally of the number of characteristics that are seen. There are many times however when, before something can be tallied, the examiner must first determine whether it exists and even what it is, that is, evidence prints and exemplar prints are not always clear. When they are not, it is necessary for the examiner to decide whether some feature is indeed a ridge characteristic or rather an anomaly caused by some factor such as debris on the surface, improper inking of the skin, or distortion. These same factors, and many others, certainly can cause the characteristics to be altered in appearance. The examiner must then decide whether what is seen is sufficiently similar to lend weight to a conclusion of identity, or whether it is only suggestive and should be given less consideration than it would deserve if it were clearer. It is these necessary determinations, which can only be made based upon the experience of the examiner, that constitute the second limitation on the ability of even the most experienced examiner to be able always to determine whether a particular print was or was not made by a particular person.

That this element of judgment exists as a necessary element of the comparison is certainly not seriously questioned. When some writers refer to the practice of identification by friction ridged skin as being an art, or as being an art and science because it has elements of both, what is being noted is the necessity for the examiner to exercise judgment based upon personal experience. Recent advances in the automation of fingerprint comparison portends well for the establishment of more objective criteria for establishing identity through friction ridge characteristics. However, the application of such criteria will still depend upon the ability of the examiner in those cases where the nature or even the mere existence of the characteristics is not readily apparent.

Given the above, the obvious question that must be addressed is What constitutes an identification? At what point can the examiner be certain that a condition of identity is fully proved? Even if the examiner is to adopt, or have imposed, some arbitrary minimum standard for a number of matching characteristics, there are still the unavoidable circumstances where the nature or existance of the characteristic must be decided by the examiner before it can be tallied and included to arrive at the "minimum number." There can be no easy answer to this dilemma.

Often, the amount of detail in a print available for comparison is more than adequate by any quantitative measure. As the number or quality, or both, of the characteristics diminish, the skill and experience of the examiner must be proportionally greater if a "correct" determination of the relationship between two prints is to be made. The accuracy of such a determination can only be judged by other examiners whose skill and specific experience will differ. Because of this, even examiners of apparently equal experience and skill may express different opinions as to whether a particular print is adequate to support a conclusive determination of identity.

Fortunately such differences are of degree; other things being equal, both examiners can actually be correct: even if some strict numerical standard is adhered to by both examiners, they must each apply their personal judgments, which at some point must differ. This dilemma is addressed in generally one or both of two ways: first, by setting a high arbitrary standard that essentially overlaps any gray areas; second, by requiring two or more examiners to agree to the results of a comparison before it is reported or given in testimony. As to the latter it would be possible to construct a situation where the results of a comparison would be determined by majority rule.

Where an examiner is, by mandate or preference, limited to reporting results by minimum numerical standard or concurrence rules, certain ethical and legal problems may arise. In the courts of the United States, and in many other countries, the final task of the examiner is to testify as an expert to his or her *own* opinion. If the examiner would personally require a smaller quantitative measure than that which has been arbitrarily set, or disagree with the conclusion of the "verifying" examiner, then the examiner could be testifying to an opinion that he or she does not truly believe. That this happens as seldom as it does is, in the author's view, due partly to the present inability to define with mathematical certainty or scientific precision the number of similarities necessary for a determination of identity. It is also due partly to the element of personal judgment and the apparent willingness of most examiners to defer to the more conservative judgment if it does not seem unreasonable.

Of course, the individual examiner must still avoid adopting the opinion of another simply because of the other's apparently greater experience or conservative predilection. The result of any comparison is the opinion of the examiner based upon training, experience, and understanding of the field. This applies as well in any of the forensic sciences.

Although excessive conservatism can overly limit the usefulness of friction ridge comparison, a measure of conservatism is important in this field as in no other. Special status seems to be afforded the practice of identification by friction skin in the courts and by the public, and it is virtually the only technique whereby a criminal defendant can be irrevocably linked to a scene or an instrument of a crime. It is therefore critically important that the examiner be as personally objective as possible and report only those conclusions which are fully justified by the evidence.

Comparing Prints

7

There are a number of factors that enter into the comparison of evidence prints to exemplar prints; the one usually considered to be the most critical is the experience of the examiner. Experience is a very broad term that encompasses many things, some of which can be taught, and some of which can be learned only by making many comparisons.

Different individuals have, of course, different perceptual abilities. One of the most obvious of these is color perception: many individuals have some degree of color vision deficiency. This is not necessarily a detriment, and under some circumstances may be advantageous due to a greater comparative sensitivity to a particular color, causing more apparent separation between an evidence print and its substrate when they are of different colors. Since most evidence prints are monochromatic (black on white or white on black), even a person who is completely "color blind" is not necessarily incapable of being a competent examiner so long as the limitations are understood and respected.

Other types of perceptual ability, the lack of which can cause difficulties, are less inherent than learned. For instance, many examiners have difficulty comparing a white or light-colored evidence print against a dark background to an exemplar print which is chromatically "normal"; others have no difficulty in these situations. It is the author's experience that some time spent studying prints of this type is usually adequate for most examiners to overcome the difficulty. The net result is a substantial savings of time that may be spent photographically "reversing" evidence prints before any comparisons can be made.

Somewhat analogous to the possible difficulties with chromatically reversed evidence prints is the problem that some (especially novice) examiners have with chemically developed evidence prints. For instance, latent prints developed with ninhydrin are actually in a paper or other absorbent substrate and many are quite faint. Such prints are usually difficult for the inexperienced examiner, and even experienced examiners may have some difficulty if they have not previously had occasion to work with such materials. Again, however, some time spent working with such prints will enable the examiner to make effective comparisons.

One of the most important things that can be taught to (or learned by) an examiner is the ability to determine the orientation of an evidence print and which part of a hand or finger made it. This can greatly reduce the amount of time necessary to make a comparison and, if success is defined as making an identification, then will also greatly increase the chance of a successful comparison. For the most part the determination of source and orientation is based upon class characteristics, including the size, shape, and ridge flow, width and spacing of ridges, and the pattern type, if any, that is present. The juxtaposition of prints can also be an important factor in any comparison that is made. These things are all characteristics which are determined by an examination of the evidence print itself.

The examiner will, at times, find it useful or even necessary to consider other factors such as the positioning of the print on an object and the size, shape, and normal use of the object. This will be helpful on those occasions when the orientation of the print and even whether it is a finger or a palm is in doubt. Taking into consideration how the object or surface would normally have been touched will often give the examiner an indication of the most likely orientation and at times even suggest the most likely hand or digit for consideration.

Orienting the Evidence Print

As has been suggested, the first task in a comparison is to determine to what the evidence print should be compared. Sometimes the choice is obvious; for instance, it is usually readily apparent whether a latent print was made by a finger or a palm. Other times it is not obvious, at least to the novice, and some amount of examination may be necessary. Occasionally, unfortunately, there is just not enough information in the evidence print even to make this basic determination.

Digits

When the evidence print represents a single digit it is often possible to determine whether it is a thumb. Thumb prints are generally larger than prints of the other digits and will often exhibit a greater distance between the center of the pattern area and the tip. Although this is certainly not infallible, after some practice the examiner will be able to determine with great accuracy that a single print is a thumb print. Determining that a particular print is not a thumb print generally requires that it be juxtaposed to other prints as part of a group. To determine that a print was made by a particular digit other than a thumb, when it is not part of a group, is generally not done with a high degree of certainty.

Certain pattern types occur with greater frequency on certain fingers than on others: whorls, for instance, are least likely to occur on little fingers and radial loops are more common on index fingers. However, if the evidence print is of a single digit, determination of which exemplar fingerprint to compare it to first are only "best guess" estimates if other prints have the same general class characterstics of pattern type, size, and shape. One particular pattern type does, however, occur almost always in a particular digit: the nutant loop is usually on a thumb and radial. Therefore, if an evidence print is a right-slope nutant loop, it was probably made by the left thumb. Figure 7.1 shows a nutant loop.

Other less distinctive pattern types are self-limiting when compared to an inked print card, in that few individuals have ten digits

Figure 7.1 Nutant loop.

that are indistinguishable in class characteristics. That more than 90% of right-slope loops are ulnar loops in the right hand is of little practical use for comparison when the exemplar prints are on the desk and the right-slope loops can be seen. It can, however, be a useful statistic when the print is to be searched through a single or even a five-finger retrieval system, allowing the most likely exemplar prints to be compared first.

Whorl patterns are somewhat similar to loops in that they generally exhibit a definite slope or flow. Right-sloping whorls, usually outer tracings, are prevalent in the right hand, and left-sloping loops, usually inner tracings, are prevalent in the left hand. As with loops, radial sloping whorls are most common in index fingers. Whorls may also exhibit a direction of rotation determinable by tracing a central spiraling ridge, or tracing the flow of loop formations in double and twinned loop-type whorls. Clockwise rotation is most prevalent in the left hand and counterclockwise in the right.

Evidence prints are often found in groups representing the simultaneous imprinting of two or more fingers. When this occurs it is often possible to determine with a high degree of accuracy (or even certainty) which fingers of which hand made the individual fingerprints. As a practical matter, such a group of prints may be considered a single print for comparison purposes. It is quite possible, even if the individual prints are inadequate for a conclusive determination of identity, that the donor can be identified based upon a comparison of the entire group.

Allowing for variations between individuals, the fingers of the hands have a fairly fixed height and length relationship. As may be seen by examining the plain or "flat" prints on a number of inked fingerprint cards, the middle finger is usually higher than the index and ring fingers and the little finger is the lowest or shortest of the fingers. These relationships often appear in evidence prints and can help the examiner determine the "class characteristic" of which finger made which print.

Figure 7.2 shows a group of prints with a particular height relationship to each other. Because the print in the center is higher than the other two it is a reasonable assumption that it was made by a middle finger. Whether the group were made by either right or left hand, the index finger would still be a radial loop. Since this is a fairly common pattern for index fingers in both hands, it would not be reasonable to attempt to assign a determination of left or right hand to this group on the basis of that pattern. If all three patterns exhibited the same slope, however, it might then be reasonable to assign a rather high probability of accuracy to the determination of which hand made the prints.

Figure 7.2 Print grouping with usual height relationship.

Figure 7.3 shows a group of latent prints with the center print higher than the prints on either side and the print on the right appearing to be lowest. Although none of the patterns can be determined with certainty, the pattern in the center print seems to have a left slope. If made by the right hand, this pattern would, then, have a radial inclination; however, in the left hand the inclination would be ulnar, which is the more common occurrence. Thus, it would be reasonable to begin the comparison of this group of prints with the assumption, if not virtual certainty, that the group was made by the index, middle, and ring fingers of a left hand.

The ability to determine which hand and finger made a particular print can be especially useful in the early stages of a comparison. For example, a great many prints have plain whorl patterns of any particular size and shape; but if it is also known that the finger of concern is the left middle finger, then a proportionately small number of even an extensive list of possible donors (suspects) will have to be compared more closely. If it is also known that the left index finger accompanying the middle finger is a radial loop, then the population of possible donors becomes very small indeed. Thus a group, not selected on the basis of their fingerprint class characteristics, can be compared and most eliminated as possible donors quite rapidly.

Because of the structure of the hand, it is possible for a group of fingerprints not to exhibit their height characteristics: the more the

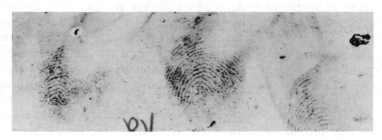

Figure 7.3 Grouping of latent prints.

Figure 7.4 Print grouping with altered height relationship.

fingers are bent, the more even they become (Figure 7.4). It is even possible, under some circumstances, for the height relationships to be reversed in a print of a group. Note that two persons may touch an object in such a manner that their prints will appear to constitute a group; caution must therefore be exercised in determining groups of prints for the purpose of search and comparison.

One factor that can be considered if when questioning whether a number of prints constitute a group is the width and spacing of the ridges. These are generally similar among the fingers although it does vary somewhat, with thumbs exhibiting the broadest ridges and the little fingers the finest. Also to be considered is the quality of the evidence prints: in a group it can be expected that the individual prints will be similar in density (darkness). The axes of the individual prints should also not be too different; this can usually be tested by comparing the prints to one's own hand.

Although the construction of the hand does not preclude finding a group of prints which includes the thumb, it does make it less likely. Such a group will usually not show a flat print of the thumb but the side of it. A flat print of the thumb on the same surface as the fingers, assuming simultaneous impressions, will usually be at an angle of greater than 90° to the axes of the fingers. Thumbs are usually found opposing the fingers, as in grasping, and may oppose flat prints of the fingers (Figure 7.5) or the side of the index finger (Figure 7.6). Unless there is a complete connection of the prints of the fingers and the thumb, as might be found around the circumference of a bottle, the inclusion of a thumb as part of a group may be less than certain. Again, the determination of whether a number of prints constitute a group may be tested by attempting to fit one's own fingers and thumb into the formation. Practical certainty that the prints constitute a group can be established when the donor is identified and, even if the prints are not individually identifiable, the class characteristics or even a small amount of individual characteristics correspond.

The shape of the finger is such that if only the tip is touched to a surface, the print is typically round and the ridges cross it approximately horizontally, or across the axis of the finger (Figure 7.7). The

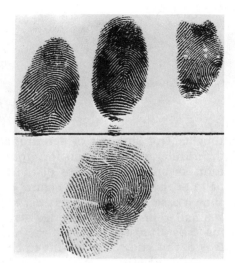

Figure 7.5 Print grouping with thumb opposing the fingers.

amount of pressure applied determines, to a degree, the size of the print as does the angle of the finger to the surface touched. Determination of the orientation of such a print is difficult at best, although the ridges tend to be somewhat coarser toward the tip, especially in the thumbs. Increasing coarseness is not a completely reliable determinant if the print is quite small; it is usually necessary to rely on other factors, such as how the object or surface would normally be

Figure 7.6 Print grouping of thumb and side of index finger.

Figure 7.7 Print grouping, tips of fingers.

touched, for any sort of determination of orientation. It is easier to determine an orientation for groups of such prints, which generally form an arc with the tips of the fingers at the convex side and the palm at the concave side (Figure 7.7). Determination of orientation in such a case can be relatively certain.

Small round prints of ridges with no distinct pattern can also be made by almost any part of the hand, not just the tips of the fingers. It is not unknown for a print to be made through a hole in a glove or for some condition of the substrate to allow only a small circular print to be made. Generally, examining the print and the surrounding area will give the examiner some indication that such may have occurred.

Prints of the medial and proximal phalanges are at times easy to determine. If the distal (end) phalange is present, even if smudged (Figure 7.8), or if a recognizable portion of palm is part of the print

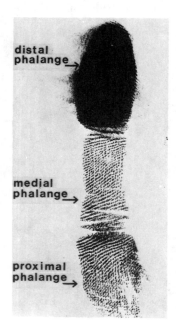

Figure 7.8 Distal, medial, and proximal phalanges.

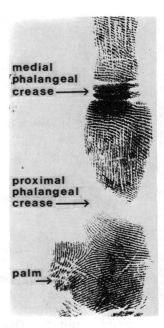

Figure 7.9 Medial and proximal phalanges and palm.

(Figure 7.9), the determination of the digit and the orientation of the print may be made with confidence. When neither of these circumstances occur, or when it is not possible to tell if part of the print is the distal phalange or palm, digit and orientation may not be determinable. It is sometimes, but not always, possible to determine, with a fair degree of confidence or even certainty, whether a small print is a medial or proximal phalange.

Ridges generally cross the medial or proximal phalanges horizontally, although they often approach verticality especially near the margin of the palm. These ridges may also exhibit patterns arching up or down (Figure 7.10), or both. Ridges here also often exhibit re-

Figure 7.10 Print of medial phalange with "arch" patterns.

Figure 7.11 Characteristic medial phalangeal crease.

markable converging or diverging ridges, and frequently possess creases along the axis of the digit. There is also a generally higher frequency of occurrence of minutiae here than on other portions of the palmar surface. The flexion creases between the margin of the palm and the proximal phalange, and between the proximal and medial phalanges also, will usually be more prominent than that between the medial and distal phalanges (Figure 7.9).

The creases marking the joints of the fingers exhibit other differences that are subject to generalization. For instance, the flexion crease between the distal and medial phalanges is more likely to be prominently doubled than the other creases; furthermore, the ridges between the creases are often distinctly unformed, appearing frequently as dots especially near the center of the digit (Figure 7.11; see also Figures 7.8 and 7.9). The flexion creases at the bases of the middle ring fingers are also more likely to be doubled than those of the index and little fingers. The crease at the base of the little finger may also show secondary creases radiating from the main crease upward and toward the near side of the hand; the same is true of the crease at the base of the index finger (Figure 7.12).

Using these as a guide may allow beginning a comparison with the most likely location and orientation of the print. The examiner should avoid fixing on one particular orientation and location unless the evidence support it is compelling. Once such a print has been compared to the most likely area in the most probable orientation without success, the examiner should, of course, peruse the exemplar prints for other areas with similar ridge flow in any orientation.

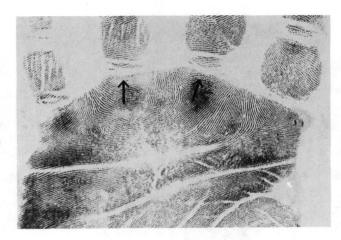

Figure 7.12
Characteristic
proximal
phalangeal creases.

Palms

Just as the digits have recognizable ridge flows, so do palm prints. These ridge flows can be generalized as class characteristics for various parts of the palm and, notwithstanding the inevitable variation that exists among individuals and even between the two palms of a single individual, it is usually possible to recognize an evidence print as having been made by a particular portion of a palm, as well as to determine its orientation.

The palm is usually divided, for classification purposes, into the thenar, hypothenar, and interdigital regions (see Chapter 3). It is possible to find evidence prints that represent all or part of each of these areas, or a combination of parts of them. On occasion, a print of a complete or nearly complete palm is found. However, an evidence print made by a palm may give every appearance of having been made by a finger (Figure 7.13), though this is uncommon.

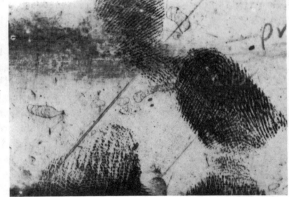

Figure 7.13 Palm prints may appear to be fingerprints.

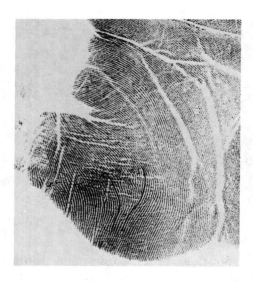

Figure 7.14 Print of the thenar: area of convergence patterns has been indicated. (See text.)

Prints of palms are usually characterized by their size; beyond that, however, novices (and even some experienced examiners) generally have difficulty determining whether the print is of a left or right palm and how it is oriented.

Thenar. The thenar area of the palm is usually composed of a field of ridges that flow in an arching pattern from top to bottom with the concave side of the arch toward the thumb. Near the center of the palm the ridges tend to become straighter and more vertical in addition to becoming somewhat narrower and more closely spaced. The ridges also become somewhat finer and more closely spaced toward the first interdigital interval between the thumb and index finger. The thenar eminence will often have an area of strongly converging ridges going toward the margin of the palm (Figure 7.14).

The first interdigital area at times possesses one of the most distinctive types of patterning to be seen on the palms (Figure 7.15). These pattern "vestiges" will appear as ridges at right angles to the general flow and sometimes as fairly squared-off loop formations. Occasionally two loop formations will be present flowing in opposite directions and, less commonly, will be whorl patterns (Figure 7.16). When a broad field of ridges possesses patterns that have very angular or square recurves, it can usually be assumed to have been made by a thenar.

More often than other parts of the palm, a print of the thenar will have an area of non-friction ridge skin printed. This is from the lower outside edge of the thumb and the flexion crease between thumb and

Figure 7.15 Patterning in the first interdigital area.

thenar may also print. If present, these represent excellent landmarks for orientation and hand determinations. One of the most common characteristics of the thenar region, which is almost always present to some degree, is creasing. Quite often these creases are quite fine and present a somewhat cross-hatched appearance. The appearance of these, though not conclusive, is strongly indicative. Other creases occur in this area which begin on the lower margin of the thenar and radiate distally, or upward. Similar creases may occur at other margins of the palm, but are more common in this region.

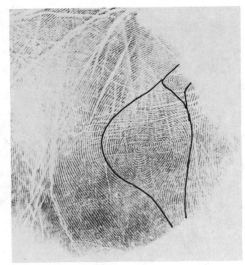

Figure 7.16 A thenar with a whorl pattern and a loop formation in the first interdigital area.

Hypothenar. The hypothenar region of the palm is, perhaps, the most commonly found palm print found in evidence prints and is often printed with part of the thenar or interdigital regions. This region usually consists of a broad field of relatively flat or slightly arching ridges which begin at approximately right angles to the axis of the palm, turn sharply upward toward the middle of the palm above the carpal delta, and turn downward toward the wrist below the carpal delta (Figure 7.17). The degree of change of slope of the ridges as they turn up or down is an excellant class characteristic. Beyond the point

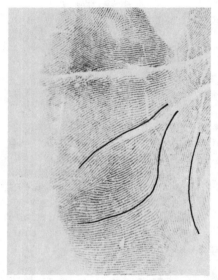

Figure 7.17 Prints of the hypothenar: areas of convergence and the finer ridges at the center of the palm have been indicated. (See text.)

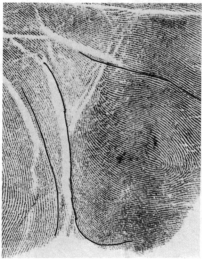

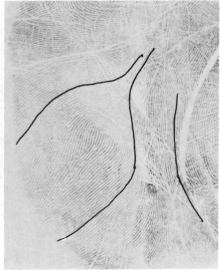

where the ridges turn, toward the center of the palm, the ridges become finer and narrower; if followed across the palm, they will begin curving into the thenar–first-interdigital region.

At about the level of the proximal transverse is usually an area of very strongly converging ridges. Here, the central vertical ridges join with the ridges from the side of the palm and flow radially toward the index finger.

A print in which the carpal delta appears is almost always possible to orient properly and distinguish left from right palm. This is so because the ridges above the delta generally turn upward more sharply than those below turn down. The finer vertical ridges at one side of the delta help determine which side is toward the middle of the palm when the delta is quite high, the convergence of ridges near the terminus of the proximal transverse crease may also be useful in determining orientation and hand accurately.

A loop found in the hypothenar is usually radial, and ridges traced from the core will exit the palm between the thumb and index finger, above the thenar. Such loops are usually accompanied by a single delta below and near the center of the palm (the carpal delta), although they may have an additional delta near the ulnar margin (as in Figure 7.18). When such loops are ulnar, with the looping ridges entering from the side of the palm below the little finger, they are usually accompanied by two deltas, one above and one below the loop (Figure 7.19).

Multiple loops originating from the same side and not forming a whorl pattern are usually radial. When these loops go in opposite di-

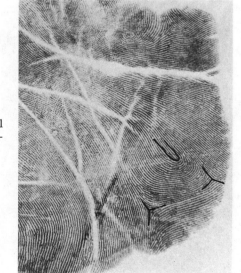

Figure 7.18 Hypothenar pattern: radial loop with two triradii. Pattern formation and triradii have been indicated.

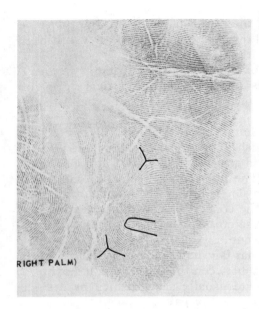

Figure 7.19 Hypothenar pattern: ulnar loop with two triradii. Pattern formation and triradii have been indicated.

rections, the narrower vertical ridges near the proximal transverse crease terminous will usually indicate the proper orientation; also, the lower loop is usually located nearer its associated delta than is the upper loop (Figure 7.20). Other loop combination patterns, whorls, and vertical arch patterns may also appear (Figure 7.21); but these, and even multiple loop patterns, occur with such low frequency that they present no practical problems when they appear.

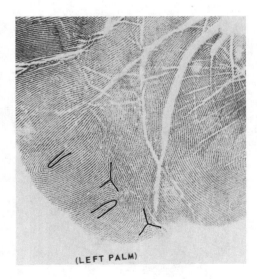

Figure 7.20 Hypothenar pattern. Ulnar and radial loops with two triradii. Pattern formations and triradii have been indicated.

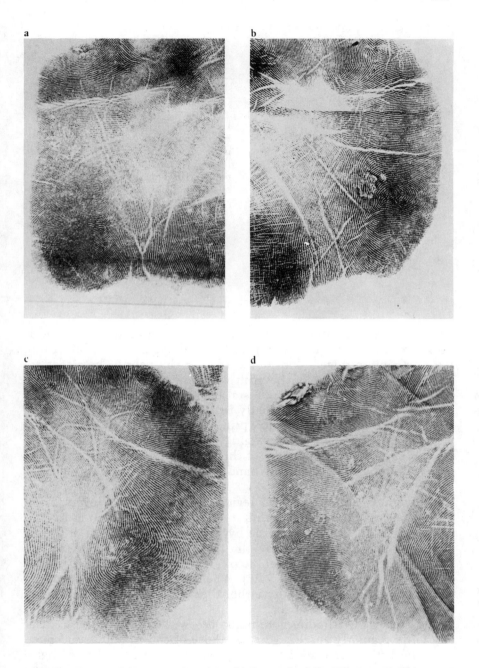

Figure 7.21 Hypothenar patterns. **a.** Double-loop whorl. **b.** Whorl. **c.** Radial nutant loop. **d.** Proximal loop.

Figure 7.22 Characteristic latent print of right hypothenar. Note that the print is narrower at the top than at the bottom, the ridges near the bottom are coarser than at the top, and the ridges "fading" out at the right side mark the ulnar margin of the palm.

The side of the palm will often appear in an evidence print and is usually characterized by the ridged skin of the hypothenar fading into the non-friction-ridged skin at the edge of the palm. The ridges toward the proximal end of the print will generally be somewhat finer (less coarse) than those at the distal end. Also, because of the shape of the hand, the print will usually be wider proximally than distally (Figure 7.22). Occasionally such prints will show the core of a loop pattern or some strongly converging ridges. Since these features are usually at or below the middle of the palm, if present they can assist in determining the most likely hand.

Interdigital. The interdigital region, just below the fingers, commonly appears in evidence prints in whole or part and often in conjunction with at least part of the hypothenar. Examination of even a few representative palm prints will quickly reveal some of the salient features of this region that can be of great assistance to the determination of orientation (Figure 7.23). When only a small portion of the region is present, it is usually either the area below the index finger or that below the little finger.

The axes of the triradius commonly below the index finger are usually fairly regularly spaced, whereas those of the triradius associated with the little finger are less evenly spaced—the two obtuse angles open downward for one and enclose the little finger flexure for the other. This is easily observed in the photographs.

Figure 7.23 Characteristic triradii below the index and little fingers. The axes of the triradii have been indicated. (See text.)

The more acute angle of the triradius below the little finger, opening toward the other fingers, often exhibits convergence of the ridges that enter from the ulnar side of the palm and those that emanate from the fourth interdigital space between the ring and little fingers. Patterning (usually a distal loop) is fairly common here, though less commonly associated with the triradius below the index finger. The distal transverse crease, or other minor creases, are often apparent in the second interdigital area between the index and middle fingers; creases are much less common in the fourth interdigital area.

The triradius below the little finger is usually located farther in from the side of the palm and the ridges radiating from it toward the side of the palm become straighter than those from the triradius below the index finger. The ridges below the triradius below the index finger are generally somewhat finer than those below the little finger triradius. Also, the ridges below the index finger triradius may be relatively straight or slightly curved, whereas those below the little finger triradius often exhibit a pronounced upward arching. The ridges toward the center of the palm from the index finger triradius are also generally somewhat straighter than those of the little finger triradius, which often exhibit quite a pronounced curvature toward the neighboring fingers.

Figure 7.24 Whorl pattern in the fourth interdigital.

Whorls in the interdigital region are more commonly located by the little finger triradius than elsewhere (Figure 7.24). The most common location for loop patterns is the third interdigital area between the middle and ring fingers.

Creases. Creases that cross the palm make excellent landmarks for orienting palm prints and, while not necessarily permanent, can be useful in many comparisons as individualizing characteristics. Their branchings and crossings can help locate minutiae and their position relative to minutiae can help support a conclusion of identity. The major flexion creases (see Chapter 3), which follow the lines where the skin of the palm folds most deeply when the hand is flexed, are relatively fixed and can be considered to be at least semipermanent features of the hand, though over time they may become more or less prominent. The amount of pressure applied during printing may also make them appear broader or narrower.

In working with evidence prints the most distinctive flexion creases commonly found are those near the carpal region between the thenar and hypothenar and the ulnar side of the distal transverse crease, which separates the hypothenar and interdigital areas. The radial longitudinal crease runs generally with the flow of the ridges from the first interdigital and around the thenar. Passing or terminating on the thenar side of the carpal delta, this crease often exhibits major branching and may, in the central palm area, be paralleled by a secondary flexion crease that passes near the carpal delta. These creases may even obscure the carpal delta. The radial longitudinal crease, near its upper terminus at the radial margin of the palm, will usually be roughly parallel with the distal transverse crease; the two

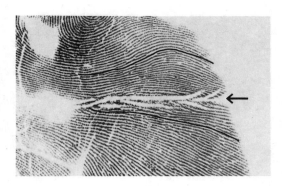

Figure 7.25 Characteristic ridge flows above and below the distal transverse crease and branching of the crease near the ulnar margin.

then diverge near the center of the palm as the radial longitudinal crease descends. These two creases will often, however, join near the radial margin of the palm. The area between them is commonly firmly creased.

The ulnar side of the distal transverse crease is usually quite distinctive, often exhibiting a number of short branchings radiating from the flexion crease toward the ulnar margin of the palm (Figure 7.25). The ridges of the hypothenar will often arch with the apices of the arches toward the crease, whereas arching of the ridges above the crease tends to be away from the crease. Often there will be quite a noticeable termination of many ridges nearly perpendicular to this flexion crease, most pronounced at about the midline of the palm (Figure 7.26). This crease is usually somewhat more pronounced near its ulnar terminus and may fade completely near the radial margin of the palm or invade the second interdigital area.

The carpal or "bracelet" creases at the juncture of the wrist and palm can usually be recognized by the friction ridges paralleling the crease on one side and the non-friction-ridged skin on the other (Figure 7.27). If the non-friction-ridged skin is recognizable as such, this is a good determinant of orientation; it is rare for ridges to parallel non-friction-ridged skin at other margins of the palm.

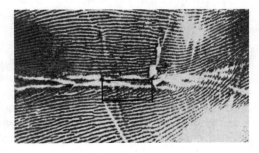

Figure 7.26 Ridges terminating vertically at the distal transverse crease.

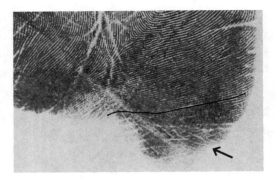

Figure 7.27 Wrist or "bracelet" creases *(arrow)*. Ridge flow above creases indicated.

Locating Minutiae

After the most likely orientation and location has been determined, class characteristics of both prints are compared to determine if they are at least similar. This examination must, of course, take into account differences in appearance that may be caused by pressure, distortion, the condition and nature of the substrate, and the printing and developing media. Once these factors have been considered, it is necessary to begin the comparison of the *minutiae*—the characteristics which make each print capable of being differentiated from any other print made by a different area of friction skin.

If a triradius or a core is clearly apparent in the evidence print, it is usually selected as a reference point. Of course, such features are formed by ridges which may be continuous, ending, bifurcated, or abutted by other ridges. Whatever their construction, these features should be the same in both prints, if so, such similarity can be considered in any final determination.

Often, however, such landmarks will not be present, or may be so poorly recorded that it is not possible to begin the comparison of minutiae at that point. Other prominent characteristics may then be used as the starting point, or reference, for the comparison. These may be areas of convergence or divergence, creases, scars, or (most likely) a small group of closely related minutiae. No matter what the quality of the prints being compared, some landmark or reference must be selected from which other characteristics can be located. Because of the variable quality of evidence prints, however, unless the reference point is considered reliable and certain to be present in the exemplar print, if it is not found, it is advisable to select another reference point and begin the comparison again.

In many evidence prints it may be quite possible to see and locate a triradius or core but, because of smudging or other defect, the nature of that landmark cannot be determined. When this occurs it is often possible to locate a reference point with respect to the landmark by distance and direction. The reference point can then be sought in the exemplar print in the same relative location. This should be done with some caution since the cause of the defect may be such that the clearer minutiae are not properly located with respect to the apparent location of the landmark. Finding the reference in the appropriate geographical location with respect to the smudged or otherwise obscured landmark can, of course, be considered in a final determination of identity. If the reference point is not found properly associated with the landmark, consideration should be given to why it was not so found: either the prints do not share a common source, or the evidence prints (or the exemplar print) is not an accurate representation of the friction ridges that made it.

A reference point can also be located by using a crease or combination of creases. Creases themselves can be considered, to an extent, to be landmarks; their direction with respect to ridge flows, their width and length, and their position with respect to other creases are all factors that can be considered. However, as mentioned earlier, creases can and do change in their appearance between prints. Although the location of major creases changes little over time, they are less reliable as landmarks than triradii and cores. Since a properly made exemplar print will deemphasize creases, and since the size and shape of the substrate and the amount of pressure applied for the evidence print can emphasize or obscure the creases, such creases will show more differences than those commonly experienced with the friction ridges. That such creases may differ from print to print is less important than how they correspond when they do appear and are similar.

If the reference point is found in both prints, then the comparison can begin in earnest. From the reference point in one print another minutiae is selected and its nature and position relative to the reference is determined. Using the relative position information, a similar characteristic is sought in the other print in the same place. For instance, in one print a bifurcation opening to the left may be separated from the reference point by two continuous ridges and may be on a line perpendicular to the ridges at the reference. Because of the possibility of distortion, the "new" characteristic may be displaced and not quite on the perpendicular line, but the number of intervening ridges should still be the same.

The comparison continues in the same manner, locating additional characteristics similar in type, orientation, and location between the two prints. If a characteristic is not found in its expected or desired location, it becomes necessary to attempt to determine whether it is absent due to some defect in the print or because the prints being compared do not share a common source. The corollary of this situation is a ridge characteristic appearing in the print where none would be if the prints shared a common source and if both prints were well recorded. When prints are of good quality such circumstances are usually resolved quickly and a conclusive determination of nonidentity reached because of the number and quality of the dissimilarities. The poorer the quality of the prints, or the greater the degree of similarity found with respect to their dissimilarities, the more the examiner must consider the possibility of a defect in one of the prints.

When comparing prints, the examiner should not take the appearance of a particular characteristic too literally. An ending ridge in one print can easily appear to be a bifurcation in another print of the same friction skin due to pressure, distortion, or other cause. Therefore, if an ending ridge is found where a bifurcation is expected, a determination of different sources for the prints being compared should be reserved until further comparison is made.

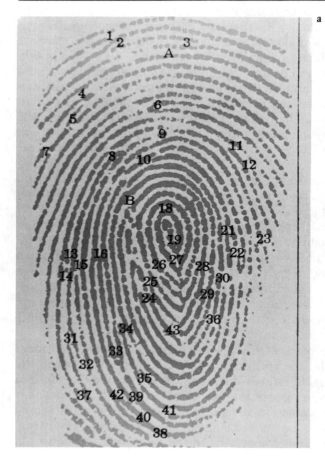

a

Figure 7.28 Galton's illustration of a change in a fingerprint: **a.** Taken in 1877; **b.** Taken in 1890.

However, additional or missing ridges in one print as compared to another should be given substantial weight in determining nonidentity. Likewise, while an ending ridge may appear to be a bifurcation on occasion, it is not reasonable for such a characteristic to "become" a continuous ridge and unlikely for it to lengthen or shorten drastically. Again, however, some minor changes in the apparent position of a characteristic can occur due to slippage, twisting, or other printing defects. It is often possible to determine that such is (or, at least, may be) the cause of the observed difference by study of the entire print.

Figure 7.28 shows two prints recorded and reported by Galton (1892). Taken several years apart, the later print exhibits a ridge near the top center of the print that was not present in the earlier print. Certainly allowances must be made for the possibility that the addi-

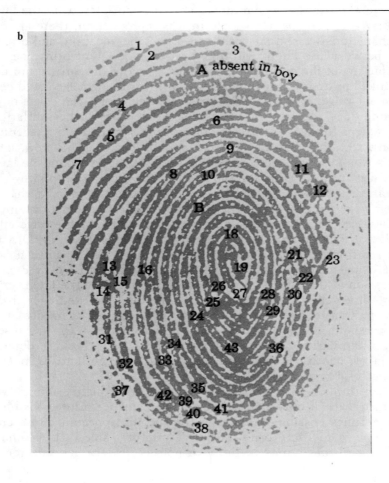

tional ridge in the later print might have been an incipient ridge that "strengthened" over the years so that it would eventually print reliably, or that some type of scarring or injury may have caused either the appearance of the ridge in the later print or the failure of the ridge to print in the earlier rendition. However, in the examples presented there is no indication of any sort that any of these circumstances prevailed; yet because of the completeness of the prints, it would be unreasonable to reach any conclusion other than that the two prints were made by the same individual. If the later print were substantially less complete, however, being only of the area with the additional ridge and having but a few ridge characteristics, it would be entirely possible to reach the erroneous conclusion that the prints were not made by the same individual.

Figure 7.29 shows a comparison of a latent print that had a similar problem. Here the inked print (b), which predated the latent print (a) by several years, shows a bifurcation that is not present in the latent print. While perhaps not visible in this reproduction, there are over 20 characteristics similar with respect to type, location, and orientation between the latent and inked prints. The latent print does not exhibit any of the normally expected indications of scarring, nor does the inked print give any indication that the missing ridge could be an incipient ridge. In spite of this lack of evidence for the cause of the missing ridge, identity was concluded on the basis of the similarities. Subsequent to the identification of the latent print, a more recent set of prints of the identified individual was located. This new set of prints was made during the same period of time in which the latent print was made and, in fact, shows the same ridge to be missing. The appearance of this more recent set of prints seems to indicate that the missing ridge was caused by a very subtle scar or a temporary injury to the skin that was just sufficient to remove the single ridge effectively without disrupting the ridges on either side. It was initially felt that scarring or temprary injury was the most likely cause for the ridge being missing, but it could also have been caused by a small depression at that location on the substrate that bore the latent print, or by some debris, or even by a lack of material on the finger at that point to transfer to the substrate. It should be emphasized that, although the examiner must give careful consideration to the cause of such dissimilarities, it will not always be certain. Besides, determination of identity is based on the presence of similarities, not the absence of dissimilarities.

When prints being compared are of very good quality and are well recorded, even if only a small area of the evidence print is visible, it is sometimes possible to consider the specific appearance of a characteristic in addition to its general descriptor (Table 7.1). An ending ridge, for instance, may be blunt or pointed or terminate nearer the

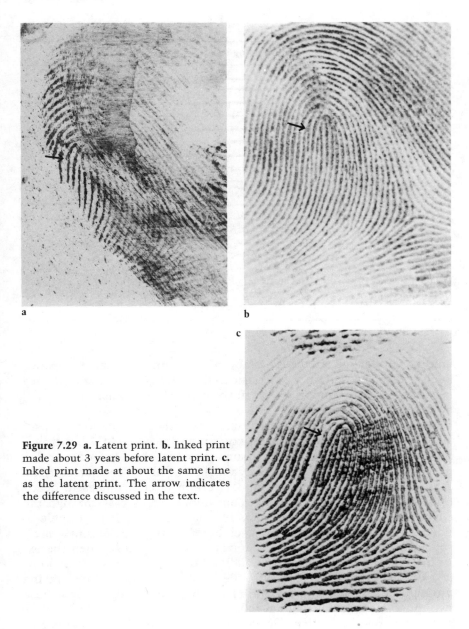

Figure 7.29 a. Latent print. **b.** Inked print made about 3 years before latent print. **c.** Inked print made at about the same time as the latent print. The arrow indicates the difference discussed in the text.

a

b

c

ridge on one side than the other. If this is apparent in the prints being compared, then the characteristic may be given more weight in the determination of identity than otherwise. To determine nonidentity on such a basis, the examiner would have to have a *substantial* de-

Table 7.1 Variations in Appearance of the Minimum Characteristic Form

Bifurcation	Ending Ridge	Dot

gree of confidence in the accuracy of both prints being compared. Such things can certainly be considered in any comparison, but they become especially important when the evidence print has but a small number of characteristics.

Occasionally, the area where a characteristic must be located will be obscured so that the characteristic cannot be seen. At other times, the location can be seen even though it is not possible to determine the nature of the characteristic. Even when a particular characteristic cannot be seen, it is possible under certain circumstances to determine that something other than continuous ridges pass through the affected area. For example (on a very small scale): if it is possible to trace two ridges that are next to each other through the obscured area, beyond which the ridges are separated by another ridge, then the examiner can be certain that the additional ridge either ends or joins one of the bracketing ridges in the obscured area. If after tracing through the affected area there are *two* intervening ridges, then those two must end in some fashion in that area.

It is not necessary that the two ridges that are traced be next to each other, any number of intervening ridges may be used. The number of intervening ridges at the end of the trace *may* indicate the number of ridges that terminate or begin in the obscured area. There are some hazards associated with this technique and the examiner must exercise sound judgment when interpreting the results. It is possible, of course, for entire characteristics such as short ridges, islands, and dots to be obscured by even a small smudged area and not be indicated by through-tracing. Also, the more intervening ridges used at the beginning of the trace, or found at its end, the greater the number of bifurcations and ending ridges that can occur in the obscured area and not be detected. For instance, a single intervening ridge at the beginning and end of a trace could be caused by a continuous ridge, or by a ridge entering the obscured area from each side and ending in some fashion. A ridge characteristic located by through-tracing would certainly not be given the same weight or consideration as one that was clearly visible; it can, however, be considered as additional evidence of the common source of two prints and may, in fact, be sufficient to allow a higher degree of certainty to be expressed.

Figure 7.30 shows a latent palm print that was affected, when lifted, by the presence of small particles of grit. These caused small white spots with black dots at their centers. Careful ridge tracing indicates that some type of ridge formation must occur at the indicated spots: however, it is not possible to determine whether, without the defects, the characteristics would manifest as ending ridges, bifurcations, or a combination of these. When compared to an inked print of the same palm such characteristics can be considered to be similar only in that "something" occurs at the appropriate place. These types of similarity would not be given as much weight in the determination of identity as they would receive if they were clearly printed, but they still would be considered.

Evidence prints will at times show only small areas of clear detail, with an insufficient amount of minutiae in the individual areas clearly printed to effect an identification. It is often possible to con-

Figure 7.30
Obscured minutiae. The areas discussed in the text are circled.

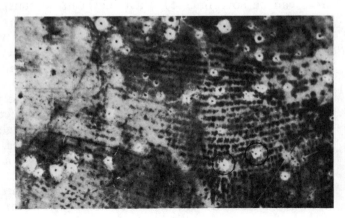

Figure 7.31 Latent print divided by a depression in the substrate.

nect such areas by carefully tracing the ridges that are present. The tracing will sometimes be quite circuitous and may involve following one ridge for a distance, counting across a number of ridges around the periphery of an unclear area, and continuing the tracing on another ridge. If this is done, the ridges crossed to continue the trace should be carefully considered since the placement of the obscured areas may cause the ridge count to be inaccurate, due to ending ridges or bifurcations adding to or reducing the count, depending upon their direction, and the precise route taken for the count. If the smaller areas can be so connected, then they can be considered to form a cohesive print for practical comparison purposes.

Somewhat more difficult to handle is the print with such small areas that cannot be connected by tracing even the most circuitous route. If the separate areas are obviously or demonstrably part of a single print, their relationship, one to the other, may be sufficient to consider them as a unit (Figure 7.31). This is especially true if the areas are also appropriately positioned with respect to some additional feature such as a triradius or a core even though such landmark is not sufficiently distinct or traceable to either area. A small area of the evidence print that bears a significant, though not conclusive similarity to the exemplar print is often sufficient to convince the examiner to look further for similarities in appropriate relationship to what has been found. It must be cautioned, however, that a single or even a few characteristics may be found to be similarly located geographically in two prints that do not share a common source. Each grouping of characteristics that is used in such a comparison should have some *significant* similarity to the exemplar print: the more tenuous the connection between the separate areas, the greater must be the significance of the similarity between each area of the evidence print and the appropriate area of the exemplar print if a conclusion of common source is to be reached.

A more extreme example of this type of problem comparison is that involving a number of individual evidence prints, each of which is insufficient for a conclusive determination of identity. If the examiner can determine that they constitute a group of prints made by a single hand at one time, the prints can be treated as separate areas of a cohesive print, each in its appropriate geographical location, and be compared as such. Here, a proper consideration of each print will assist by adding additional class characteristics and, reducing the population of potential donors. The individual prints can also be considered as landmarks, especially if the proper finger or portion of the palm that made it can be determined and the reference points and other individual characteristics located with respect to the landmarks (see Figure 8.4, p. 198).

It is possible to utilize a number of nongroup prints in the comparison process. A single print, though not identifiable, may strongly suggest the likely orientation of other prints from the same surface which cannot be properly oriented but are sufficiently clear for identification purposes. For example, prints of the thumb are found on many items in a position of opposition to the fingers of the same hand. It is possible for a group of fingers, recognizable as such but devoid of class or individual characteristics, to be opposed to a print that, alone, would be of indeterminable origin. In such a case it might be quite reasonable to infer that the one usable print is a thumb and, therefore, know its orientation and the part of the thumb that made the print. Using such information, it is then necessary to locate a reference point and begin the comparison. In this case, even though a direct connection may be lacking between the opposing prints, such prints can also be considered a group for comparison and identification purposes.

Prints from several surfaces may be found that individually lack sufficient class and individual characteristics to identify the donor, but which each show a significant degree of similarity to the exemplar material of one individual. Reaching a decision in a case such as this is difficult in the extreme. When a number of prints each exhibit a significant degree of similarity to the prints of a known individual, but each is lacking in some respect, the examiner must decide whether the *sum* of the individual significances is sufficient to establish identity.

Tonally Reversed Prints

The latent print examiner will occasionally have to compare an evidence print that is tonally reversed. This is a print that is caused by the development of the furrows of a portion of friction skin rather than the ridges. The tonally reversed print is differentiated from a print that is developed with a light-colored powder and preserved on a dark background because in that case it is known from the outset that the ridges are light and the furrows dark. In the case of a tonally reversed print, the intention was usually to cause the ridge to develop to a dark color, although the opposite occurred.

Tonal reversals should be anticipated when the background collects so much powder that it appears as dark as the dark lines within the boundary of the friction skin print (Figure 7.32). Careful inspection of the print may reveal the openings of the pores as dark spots along the light-colored spaces. If the pores can be seen in the light lines, then the print is certain to be a tonal reversal. Care must be taken to not interpret randomly scattered powder as pores. The nature of evidence prints is such that pores are not reliably printed, so this is not always possible to apply. Often, the existence of a tonal reversal cannot be determined until it is compared to another print from the same source. When this is done the examiner will usually note that where a bifurcation exists in one print, an ending ridge appears in the other. Islands in one print appear as short ridges in the other. Unless the evidence print is well recorded, however, even these distinctions can be obscured.

Tonal reversals are most noticeable about the core and delta areas

Figure 7.32 Tonal reversal. The print on the right is reversed, the print on the left is partially reversed.

where the ridges change direction. In the core area, an innermost re-curve or staple with no enclosed rods will, in the tonally reversed print, appear as a recurve with a single rod enclosed. In fact, there will always be one more or one less apparent rod in the core of a reversed print than the unreversed print. This but can only be deter-mined when the evidence print is compared to the appropriate inked print.

In the delta area, tonal reversals are distinguished by the presence of a bifurcation opening toward the core in one print whereas the other print shows no ridges connecting at that point. A dot at the delta of one print will appear as a light area in the other print sur-rounded by three connecting ridges that radiate along the axes of the triradius.

In tonally reversed prints, triradii and cores are, of course, not al-ways visible, being smudged or otherwise obscured. In these instances the tonal reversal should be suspected when there is a gain or loss of a ridge count between groups of minutiae on opposite sides of these landmarks.

The latent print on the right of Figure 7.32 is a classic reversal: the ridges are light and show good pore detail and the scar which is white in the corresponding inked print (Figure 7.33a) is dark in the latent print. The latent print on the left is *not* reversed completely with the majority of the print being black ridges on a white background. The print on the right in figure 7.33b is a latent print which was made by the same finger that made the print on the left in Figure 7.33a. Here the print is also not totally reversed, with the area just to the left of the delta on the right being composed quite clearly of dark ridges on a light background. The left side of the print seems to be reversed, showing very thin dark lines separated by broad light ridges. If the ridges near the bottom recurve are carefully traced in a counterclock-wise direction, it will be seen that the dark ridges on the right grad-ually become lighter than the separating spaces. What is occurring is that, at about the midpoint between the upper and lower recurves, the dark lines begin to delineate just the edges of the ridges; this can cause a print to appear reversed and cause some characteristics to seem displaced when they are not. Extreme care is necessary to trace ridges accurately in cases such as this.

Not all prints that appear in dark fields are tonal reversals: some such prints occur when a substance on the substrate collects on the ridges and is redeposited by the ridges after a very little movement. Thus, material is removed from the surface and redeposited, causing a print that appears to be a tonal reversal but is not.

Nor are all tonally reversed prints in a dark field. Occasionally the substance that is transferred from the skin to the substrate comes not from the ridges but from the valleys, between the ridges. This may

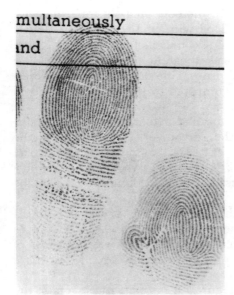

multaneously

ınd

a

Figure 7.33 Tonal reversal. **a.** Inked prints of the fingers that made the latent prints in (**b**) and those in Figure 7.32. **b.** The print on the right is partially reversed.

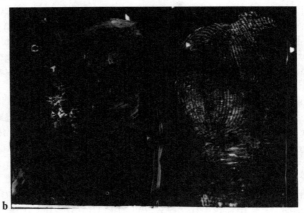

b

happen with inked prints (Figure 7.34) when skin is inked excessively and then printed repeatedly until the only ink that is left is between the ridges and the final print appears to be good. The same effect can be caused by any substance, including perspiration or sebum.

The first indication of a potential reversal may be nothing more than an inability to resolve some nonspecific problem in tracing or counting. When this occurs the examiner should carefully trace the ridges around and through the bothersome area. Usually this will reveal the boundary of the reversed area and the point at which the ridges begin changing from dark to light, resolving the difficulty.

Partial reversals can be caused by the previously mentioned slip-

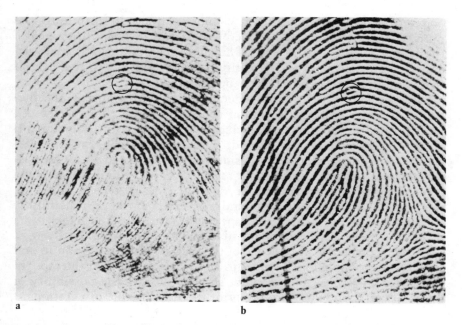

Figure 7.34 a. Tonally reversed inked print. **b.** Properly made inked print of the same finger. Note the appearance of the short ridge in the circle.

ping and redeposition. When this occurs the reversed area will be in the area of the ridges that cross the direction of slippage. Often, ridges that flow in the direction of slippage will be completely obscured; when they do print they may show an extraordinary amount of elongation and displacement of minutiae. Islands can appear simply as broad ridges, being filled in or smudged, and one bifurcation of the feature slides over the other. Dots can appear as short ridges, and a bifurcating ridge can appear much broader in front of the bifurcation. The additional length of short ridges and dots, as well as the length of the broadened ridges preceding bifurcation, can indicate the amount of slippage that has occurred.

Laterally Reversed Prints

Lateral (left-to-right) reversals are as rare as might be expected. Although it is theoretically possible for latent print material to transfer from one surface to another and still be capable of development, the author has never experienced it in practical work with evidence prints. Nevertheless, some situations do occur in which the examiner must deal with a print that is essentially backward.

One example of this is an evidence print found inside a transparent object in a position such that it cannot be lifted. In examining the print, therefore, it must be treated as a lateral reversal. In this case, the lateral reversal is definitely known as such and can be managed easily: the usual method for rectifying such prints is to photograph them and then print the negative upside down.

Lateral reversals also occur when working with transparent adhesive materials. This is a common concern when a print, developed with ninhydrin, appears under clear adhesive tape on a document. Since it is possible for the ninhydrin to develop a print on the adhesive as well as on the paper, consideration must be given to the possibility that the print is laterally reversed. Close examination of the print may show that it extends beyond the adhesive tape. If this is so, the print is certain not to be laterally reversed. If the print definitely extends just to the edge of the tape and no further, it is likely to be reversed. Often, it will not be possible to determine whether the print terminates precisely on the edge of the tape or extends beyond it, and it is just as possible for the print to appear entirely under the tape. In these circumstances the examiner should consider the possibility of lateral reversal and compare the print in both possible orientations.

Distortion

Distortion can be caused by a number of factors: slippage, pressure, rotation (circular slippage), and even the shape of the substrate can cause the evidence or exemplar print to vary in appearance from an optimal recording of the frictional ridges.

The more pressure applied when making the print, and the greater the amount of material (if any) transferred, the broader the ridges will appear. The broadening can cause a ridge ending to appear to touch a ridge passing next to it and, in extreme cases, may make it appear to touch the ridges on both sides. Sufficient force applied to the skin in a direction other than straight down can also cause apparent connections where none should exist. The shape of the fingers and palms, the shape of the surface touched, and the attitude or angle of the finger or palm as it contacts the substrate can cause different amounts of pressure over different parts of the skin that contact the surface. Therefore, one part of a print may exhibit overly broad ridges and abscured ridge endings whereas another part, made with less than optimum pressure, exhibits just the opposite effects of narrow ridge and obscured, unprinted ridge connections.

Incipient ridges may appear in one print and not another due to varying pressure when the prints are made. Such characteristics, which may not appear at all in a lightly made print, appear as fine dots with more pressure and as lines connecting what were dots with a substantial amount of pressure. Because they are unreliably present, the absence of such features in one print of a pair with otherwise substantial agreement is usually not a matter of concern. Where they are present in both prints they can certainly be considered as additional evidence of identity.

Slippage is movement of the skin while in contact with the substrate in a straight line or rotationally. The effects of slippage can be obvious elongation of ridges that flow in the direction of slippage, and smudging, blurring, and even tonal reversal of those ridges that cross the direction of slippage. Slippage can also cause the print to become fainter due to the greater distribution of the limited material of the deposit. Ridges that parallel the direction of travel may appear quite narrow.

Rotational slippage can cause the same effects as straight-line slippage; ridges farthest from the epicenter of the rotation, however, undergo a greater linear displacement than those nearer the center. Rotational distortion of an area of friction ridges that is composed of essentially straight ridges will usually obscure the entire print. If, however, the ridges are curved, as in a whorl or near a loop core, the minutiae may be quite usable even if substantially displaced.

It is quite possible for only a part of a print to be affected by slippage: only part of the finger or palm may be in contact with the substrate when the slippage occurs, after which greater pressure or a change of angle of the digit or palm brings a new area of skin into contact with the surface. It is also possible for one area of skin contacting the substrate to have sufficient pressure to allow it to remain relatively fixed while another area slides across the surface. Good

Figure 7.35 Comparison of a distorted print. The reference group is indicated by the rectangle.

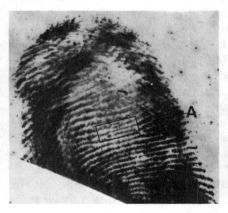

Figure 7.36 Comparison of a distorted print. The reference group is indicated by the circle.

firm contact of the digit or palm after the slippage has occurred can yield a good print in spite of the slippage.

Figures 7.35 and 7.36 show good examples of the effects of slippage.

Overlain Prints

Prints will often be found that would obviously be useful but for the existence of another print at the same place. If one print is substantially darker than the other, however, the darker print may sometimes be easily compared. Even if both prints are of the same density, it may still be possible to sort them out in areas where the ridge flows of the two prints are at right angles. Where the flows of the ridges coincide is where most of the difficulty in tracing and locating minutiae occurs if the area is not totally obscured; persistence and caution are required in such cases. The author does not believe that overlain prints can "combine" in such a manner that it would be possible mistakenly to identify the wrong individual as a donor. The most likely occurrence is that the donor or donors would be excluded because of anomalous characteristics or apparent shifts in the location of characteristics caused by the second, perhaps unnoticed, print.

Two prints will occasionally knit quite neatly together giving the appearance of a single print as in Figure 7.37. The prints may be from

Figure 7.37 Comparison of overlain prints. The reference point is indicated by the circle.

different donors but such prints usually from the same donor are printed by the same digit or part of the palm. This type of print usually represents a print made by the skin making contact, the pressure being released, the skin moved a very short distance, and contact being reestablished.

When this does occur it is usually possible to determine the line at which the prints join and even the degree and direction of shift by careful examination. The line at which the prints join is usually distinguished by a significant series of broadened or slightly overlapped ridges. The line may be darker than the ridges on either side or the ridges on one side darker than the ridges on the other side of the line. This, of course, will occur only when the joining is perpendicular to the flow of the ridges.

If the two prints are joined parallel to the ridge flows as in Figure 7.37, it may not be possible to determine the precise line of connection between the prints. When this happens, and it is fortunately rare, the examiner will have little in the way of objective, demonstrable evidence that the print seen is caused by more than a single, cohesive area of friction ridged skin. Here, the examiner will have to address the question: Given the degree of similarity that is observed, what could have caused the anomalous positioning of the characteristics? If slippage and "knitting" is a reasonable possibility, even though not conclusively demonstrable, it may still be possible to reach a determination of identity if the degree of similarity between the prints being compared is sufficiently significant.

Some Comparisons of Evidence Prints

8

FIGURE 7.35 (p. 187)
The latent print in this case shows no pattern type which can be used as a class characteristic. While no pattern type is discernable, the print is certainly a finger and the distance between the lowest part of the print and the tip suggests that the print is likely to have been made by a thumb. Although many of the ridge characteristics are blurred, those in the center of the print are quite clear and can be used easily as reference points in a number of combinations. The group selected as a reference is the short ridge and the short bifurcation (or short ridge) in box **A**. From this reference can be located two ending ridges which are below **A** and separated from it by one continuous ridge. The fourth ridge count above the short bifurcation of **A** is a ridge ending on the left; above that and slightly overlapping it is a ridge ending on the left, and above *that* and slightly overlapping it is a ridge ending on the left.

In the inked print can be seen an ending ridge just three counts above the short bifurcation of **A**. At the same location in the latent print can be seen a very blurred rendition of the same characteristic which appears more like a bifurcation than an ending ridge.

Some distortion is obvious here. The clearest ridges in the latent print appear virtually straight whereas those of the inked print are obviously curved. The ridges at the center of the latent print broaden toward the edges of the print but those of the inked print do not. The smudging around the edges of the latent print and the broadening ridges near the edges indicate that the print was made with some pressure probably in a direction along the axis of the print; this is more than adequate to account for the lack of curvature and for an ending ridge that appears to be a bifurcation.

FIGURE 7.36 (p. 188)
Perhaps the first thing noticeable here is the difference in the shapes of the two prints. The latent print exhibits complex curvature of the ridges to the right of the upright loop whereas the inked print shows ridges that are smoothly curved. Also to be noted is that the ridges to the left of the upright loop in the latent print are spaced farther apart than those to the right; the inked print shows no such difference. The nature of latent prints is such that this type of distortion, although perhaps exaggerated here, is not uncommon. Of more importance to the examiner are the class characteristics of pattern type (double loop whorl) and size or approximate distances between the landmarks present in the latent print—the upper and lower recurves and the right delta. These class characteristics are sufficiently similar to those of the inked print that the comparison should continue to the comparison of the ridge characteristics.

An excellent reference for the start of the comparison is the group of characteristics on the left side of the upright loop (in circle **A**). A similar group of characteristics is found in the inked print in the appropriate place although the characteristics in the latent print appear broader than those of the inked print. If the ridge bearing the middle feature of the reference group, which is a very small island, is carefully traced down and toward the right delta, it will be found to come within two ridge counts of the delta. In the inked print the delta appears as a dot whereas in the latent print there appear to be a connection between the "dot" and the upper type line. Without actually examining the finger of the individual it would not be possible to determine whether the difference is due to too much pressure in the latent print, too little pressure in the inked print, or some other cause. The features that are seen, however, are sufficiently similar to cause no problem in continuing the comparison.

Just to the right of **A** in the inked print a bifurcation can be seen; in that position in the latent print is a feature that could be either a bifurcation or an ending ridge. The fifth ridge count to the right of that feature is another ending ridge. If that ridge is traced going back up, it can be seen that there is a bifurcation on the ridge just to the left of it. The same features appear in both prints in the same orientation and relative position. Many more similarities can be found by carefully tracing the ridges between the upright loop and the right delta.

The astute examiner will have noted by careful examination of the prints that there are some characteristics in the latent print that are not in the inked print. For instance, in the latent print the second ridge to the left of the reference group ends a short distance below it, and there is an island or bifurcation on the ridge just to the right of the reference group, neither of which appear in the inked print. It will be recalled that the latent print has been subjected to a significant degree of distortion. Also to be observed is a blurred area above the upright loop that curves around and to the right of the print. If this area is closely examined and continued down and to the left, it will be seen to continue to the area of the "new" ending ridge. Examination of the area above and to the left of the upright loop shows a number of overlapping ridges which may not be apparent in this reproduction. These factors indicate that this latent print has been affected by some slight overlapping of two prints of the same finger, which is more than adequate to account for the anomalous characteristics.

FIGURE 7.37 (p. 189)
In this comparison the class characteristics are fairly clear, the two prints being small count right-slope loops. The core area provides a good reference—a recurve with a single rod enclosed. As in Figure 7.36, the latent print has been affected by the overlaying of two prints of the same finger. It can be easily seen that the dot at **A** in the latent print is three ridge counts from the delta whereas a similar feature in the inked print is five ridge counts from the delta. That this is caused by the overlaying of two prints is evidenced by the numerous slightly overlapping ridges directly above the core in the latent print. To the left of a line drawn from this area of overlapped ridges down and just outside the delta, all of the minutiae are properly placed with respect to the dot; to the right of that line, the minutiae are properly located with respect to the core of the print.

It is obvious from just a cursory examination of the latent print that there are, in fact, a number of latent prints. There are, in the photograph here, at least five and possibly six separate prints (including the two in the overlain print identified). When this occurs the examiner should anticipate the potential for more than one print appearing to be a single print.

FIGURE 8.1
This comparison involves a much more extreme example of overlain prints: a case, not just of displaced characteristics, but of a complete change of the appearance of the class characteristics of the prints. Due to the overlapping of two prints, the latent print appears to be a whorl pattern with an elongated core. The two prints that were subsequently identified were a loop and a whorl pattern with a very small circular core area. The key to this identification was the examiner just happening to notice the "trifurcation" above and to the right of the right delta in the latent print and a similar characteristic

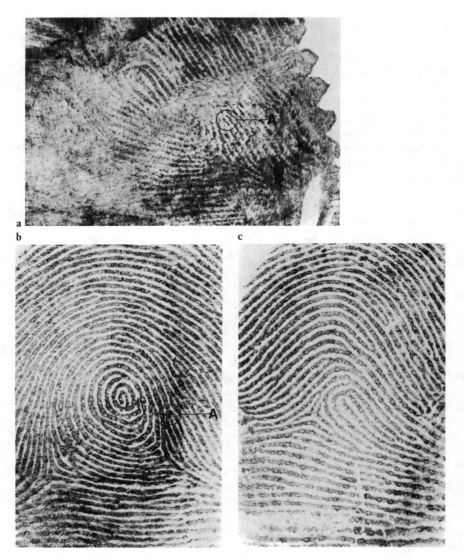

Figure 8.1 Comparison of overlain prints. The reference point for one print in the comparison is indicated by the circle in (a) and (b). Note the shape of the upper recurve formation in (a) and the core area of (c).

in the inked print of the whorl pattern (**A**). Fortunately, both prints were made by the same hand of one individual. The overlapping region of these prints is the light area above the trifurcation and, from where that crosses the looping formation, down and to the left.

FIGURE 8.2

Even though seemingly lacking in significant class characteristics, the size and shape of this latent print are such that it is certain that the print was made by a finger. The direction of the ridges near the lower right margin suggest that there may be a delta in the pattern which was unprinted, and the slope of the ridges near the center of the print is characteristic of a left-slope loop. The initial evaluation of this print is therefore that it is probably a left-slope loop, may be a tented arch and that it is highly unlikely, although possible, that it is another pattern such as a double loop or accidental whorl.

A useful reference group (**A**) are two ending ridges separated by one continuous ridge. A similar group is found in the inked print. Below **A** to the right and separated by a single ridge is another ending ridge in the latent print; a similar characteristic can be located in the inked print. Three ridge counts above **A** are a pair of overlapping ridges which appear in both prints: the first of these ends on its lower end and the second ends on its upper end. With this type of characteristic, especially when the overlap is as short as this and when the ridges are so close, it is possible for the characteristic to appear as a very short bifurcating ridge or spur. It is also quite possible with very little smudging or excess pressure for the feature to be completely obscured, appearing as a single, continuous ridge.

In this case the inked print shows some amount of incipient ridges which manifest as numerous dots between the ridges. It will be noted that these dots are not visible in the latent print. The nonappearance

Figure 8.2 Comparison. The reference group is indicated by the circle.

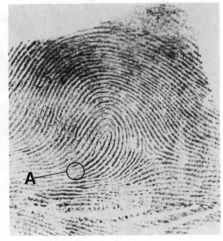

of such incipient ridges is of little consequence because they are generally unreliably printed even with inked prints. Incipient ridges have no pores to exude perspiration, so that for them to print in a latent print they would have to have been coated with perspiration from the ridges or with sebum from some other part of the body or some other contaminant. When the skin is inked for making exemplar prints, the incipient ridges will be inked if they are as high as the ridges or if enough pressure is applied to compress the ridges far enough to allow the incipient ridges to ink. When such incipient ridges do appear in both prints being compared they can be used for the determination of identity just as can the ridges.

FIGURE 8.3
In this case the pattern type of the latent print is easily determined to be a right-slope loop although the delta is unprinted and the core is unclear. Although unclear, the core of the latent print can be used as a landmark to locate, approximately, the short ridge at **A**. A short ridge appears in the inked print in the same relationship to the core of the print. Above the feature at **A** in the latent print at the second

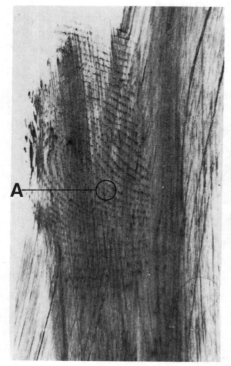

Figure 8.3 Comparison. The reference group is indicated by the circle.

count to the right is what appears to be an ending ridge and in the inked print in the same relative location is what appears to be a bifurcation. It can be seen that the ridges in the inked print are closer together than those of the latent print and, although it is not possible to determine which is the most accurate representation of the skin that made the prints from these examples, the difference in ridge spacing could easily account for an ending ridge appearing as a bifurcation or vice versa if it is caused by distortion and not by the prints being made by different donors.

Four ridges to the right of **A** in both prints is an ending ridge; if the ridge four ridges to the right of that is traced upward, it can be seen to end in the same relative location in both prints.

FIGURE **8.4**

This is a comparison that even a novice examiner would find relatively easy. The latent prints show excellent class characteristics. Since the apparent slope of the prints is to the left and the direction of rotation of the ridges is clockwise, this group of prints can be compared with the beginning assumption that they were made by the left hand. If, once the comparison is begun, the prints cannot be identified with those particular fingers of the potential donor, they should certainly be compared to the other fingers.

The latent print on the right shows what may be a scar on the right side just below the core area, but this should be considered only lightly as a class characteristic for two reasons: (1) it could easily be nothing more than a defect in the latent print and (2) the inked prints may have been made before the finger was scarred.

Even as well recorded as these prints appear to be, it is well to note that there are still features whose appearance differs between the inked and the latent prints. For instance, at **A** in the latent print is what clearly appears to be an ending ridge; the corresponding feature in the inked print is just as clearly a bifurcation.

FIGURE **8.5**

The group of latent prints shown here were developed, unfortunately, with black powder on a cardboard surface. Received in this condition with tape already placed over the prints to preserve them, there was no choice but to work with the prints as they appeared. The relationship of the three prints to each other and the slope of the ridges indicates that the prints were made by the index, middle, and ring fingers of a right hand. The index and middle fingers are right-slope loops and the ring finger appears to be, probably, a small whorl pattern. The three inked prints of the index, middle, and ring fingers of the right hand of a suspected donor have the same class characteristics as the latent prints to the extent that they can be determined.

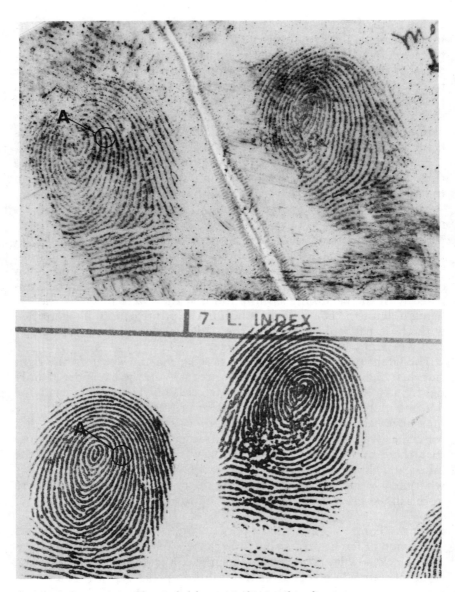

Figure 8.4 Comparison. The circled feature is discussed in the text.

(This particular group of pattern types occurs in approximately 10% of the population; considering the pattern sizes, the number of potential donors is certainly no more than a few percent of the total population.)

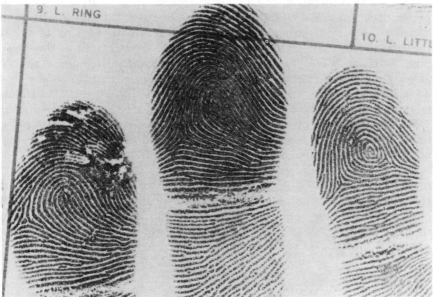

Figure 8.5 Comparison (a group of fingers). To avoid obscuring any detail, reference points have not been indicated. See the text for discussion.

The reference point for the index finger **A** is a bifurcation located below the core that opens upward. From this can be located a bifurcation eight ridges to the left which opens downward, enclosing the dot which is the delta for the pattern. To the left of that bifurcation are two ending ridges, one above and one below it.

For the middle finger there is an ending ridge located three counts to the left of the core in the inked print and a similar feature appears in the latent print three ridges to the left of the apparent location of the core. This can be used as the reference point. Tracing this ridge down in the inked print, a very small island or an enlarged pore can be seen at a point just opposite the delta. In the latent print the ridge appears simply to bulge at the same relative location. Continuing the trace for a short distance and then counting down three ridges, an ending ridge can be located that, in the inked print, passes in front of the delta. An ending ridge appears in the same relative location in the latent print.

In the ring finger in the inked print, a large island can be seen two ridge counts to the left of the core. Just to the left of the upper bifurcation of this island there is an ending ridge. In the latent print there is a very distinct bifurcation opening upward which could correspond to the lower bifurcation of the island. Where there should be the upper bifurcation and an ending ridge, the latent print appears to have continuous ridges with a small dot between them. Bearing in mind the nature of latent prints in general and the roughness of the cardboard surface, it is easy to understand how the features could appear as they do. All of the necessary elements are present to consider this a similarity, although it should not be given as much weight or consideration as it might deserve if more accurately recorded. Another similarity in this print can be located as the second ridge count to the left of the lower bifurcation of the island. This is an ending ridge which is similarly located in both the inked and latent prints.

In this case it is uncertain whether any one of the individual latent prints is sufficient to support a conclusion of identity. However, if the prints are considered as a group, with all of the appropriate class characteristics and a significant number of similarities of minutiae, the identification is as certain as can be obtained with a single print of good quality.

FIGURE **8.6**

This presents a case in which the precise orientation of the latent print could not be determined from an examination of just the latent print. The palm identified was one with a class characteristic of a very high carpal delta. Because of this, the ridges below the delta show a convergence that is similar to that which may be encountered above the delta near the center of the palm in the area of the termi-

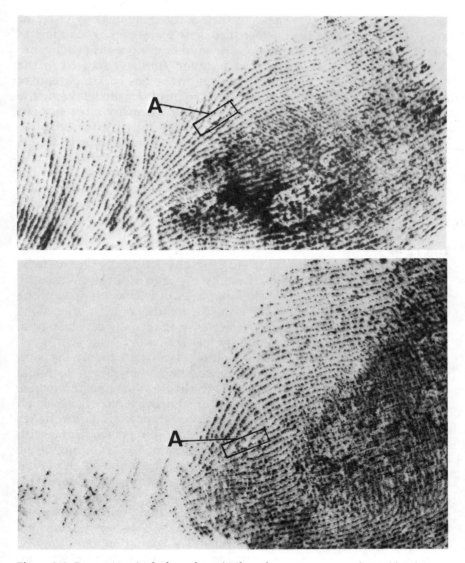

Figure 8.6 Comparison (right hypothenar). The reference group is indicated by the rectangle.

nation of the proximal transverse crease. Although made by a right palm in the orientation shown, if rotated 180°, the latent print would appear to have been made by a left palm.

For locating a reference group the area of greatest convergence serves well; the group selected here (**A**) is two ending ridges and a bifurcation. The bifurcation opens to the right, the ridge above it ends just to the left of the bifurcation, and the ridge above that ends just a bit farther to the left. Because of the spotty character of the latent print it is appropriate to consider that these features may manifest as either ending ridges or bifurcations in another print of the same palm. A similar group of characteristics is found similarly located in the inked print at **A.** Just below **A** in both prints can be seen a pair of overlapping ridges with the ridge which comes from the left being the upper ridge in the overlapped formation. A great many more similarities can be located by counting ridges and carefully tracing them.

The reader will have noticed that the latent print is more complete than the inked print in this case. Although unfortunate, this is a common occurrence when the individuals who prepare the inked prints are unaware of proper printing procedures. The inked print was also quite light due to insufficient inking and light pressure which caused the rather spotty appearance.

FIGURE **8.7**

This latent print exhibits sufficient class characteristics for one to be able to determine that it was made by the thenar of the right palm. The curvature of the lower margin of the print is characteristic of the lower margin of the thenar. The general curvature of the ridges, along with the area of strongly converging ridges, makes the determination of hand, location, and orientation quite certain.

Because of the large number of ending ridges and bifurcations commonly found in an area of convergence, the author prefers to find a reference somewhat away from this area in cases such as this where there is large area printed. Using the area of convergence as a landmark it is possible to locate a great many groups of characteristics which are suitable to use as landmarks. On a line perpendicular with the flow of the ridges, below and to the right of the beginning of the convergence and some distance from it, can be found in the latent print what appear to be two dots. Following down in the same space in which the dots appear is an ending ridge. A similar, though not identical configuration can be found in the inked print in a similar relative location at **A.** In the inked print there is a short ridge where there are two dots in the latent prints. This variation can easily be caused by differences in pressure and is, at this point, inconsequential. Four ridges to the right of the short ridge or dots in both prints are two overlapping ridges. The comparison continues in the same manner, locating additional characteristics and relating them to what has already been found.

The comparison could as easily be started at **B,** two short ridges separated by a single ridge. Here the comparison might be continued by tracing the intervening ridge up to the short bifurcation which opens upward and noting the bifurcation just to the left which opens downward.

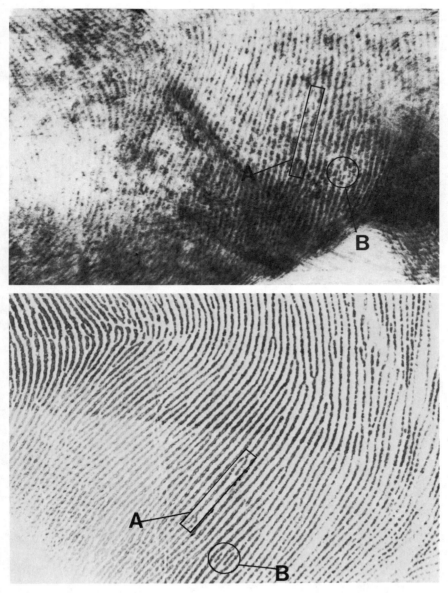

Figure 8.7 Comparison (right thenar). The reference groups are indicated by the rectangle and the circle.

FIGURE **8.8**
As in Figure 8.7, this latent print is a print of the thenar of a right hand. Although not as complete as the previous print this also shows the characteristic curvature of the thenar. The direction of the con-

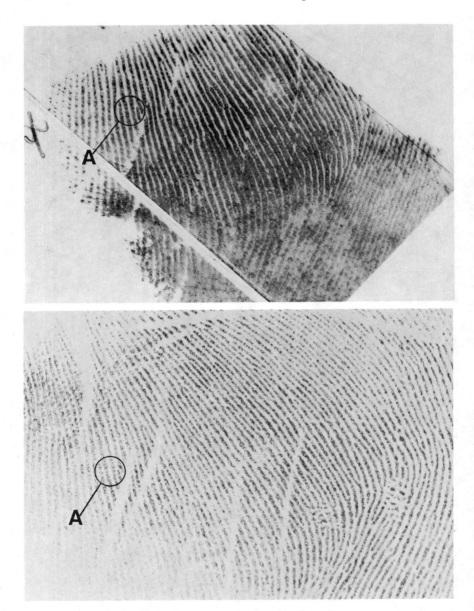

Figure 8.8 Comparison (right thenar near the thumb). The reference group is indicated by the circle.

verging ridges allows the determination of right hand with virtual certainty. In this comparison, the creases, which show as white lines, can be used as landmarks to locate reference points from which to begin the comparison. One possible reference group (there are many that can be used) is the short ridge and ending ridge separated by two ridges at **A.** The short ridge is just above a crease. Examining the creases in the inked print it it possible to find a similar short ridge located just above a crease and separated from an ending ridge to its left by two ridges.

This latent print, while not nearly as clear as the preceding two, is as easy to orient due to the presence of class characteristics. The shape of the print, narrower at the top than the bottom, and the flexion crease near the top are characteristic of prints of the hypothenar. The location of the triradius at the lower right, combined with the shape of the print and the distal transverse flexion crease at the top of the print, allow the determination that this print was made by the hypothenar of a left hand to be made with a high degree of certainty.

The ridge spacing, distance between the triradius (carpal delta), and the crease immediately to the left of the triradius are all class characteristics that the latent print has in common with the inked print. Because of the clarity, or lack of clarity of the two prints, this comparison presents somewhat more of a problem in locating a reference group than might be wished. Here it might be useful to locate a characteristic such as **A,** which appears to be an island in the latent print,

Figure 8.9 Comparison (left hypothenar). The reference group is indicated by the circle.

and measure its distance from the flexion crease using calipers or a ruler. Transferring that measurement to the inked print and allowing several ridges for distortion, a similar feature is located in the inked print. Here again, because of the quality of the two prints being compared, some difference in the general appearance of the characteristic can be allowed; thus **A** in the inked print is sufficiently similar and other characteristics can be sought using these as reference points. If from these features other characteristics cannot be located in the proper relationships, then, because of the quality of the prints and the uncertainties involved in locating the reference point in the inked print, it would be necessary to find another reference point and begin the comparison process anew.

However, in this case, the reference selected is adequate and other characteristics are indeed properly located with respect to the reference. For example, the sixth ridge count above **A** is an ending ridge left and the fifth ridge count below **A** is an ending ridge right.

The handful of comparisons presented here are not meant to cover the full range of tasks that will face the examiner. Evidence prints are found that are better and worse than any seen here. Many evidence prints present problems in interpretation of orientation and location (digit or palm) to the extent that it is not possible to make any such determination and the print must be compared to the inked prints in every conceivable location and orientation. Some evidence prints are so poor that their very existence is a matter of judgment for the examiner. In every case the examiner must work in a methodical manner, give consideration to everything that is seen, and exercise sound judgment when making any determinations.

Reporting and Testifying to Conclusions

9

The identification of an evidence print, or even a set of inked prints, does *not* establish guilt or prove criminality. Finding a latent print made by an individual on a weapon used to commit homicide proves only that the individual contacted the weapon at some point in time. If the circumstances are such that the print being on the weapon is inconsistent with innocence, then it may be appropriate for the individual to be found guilty by the *courts*. The author was once asked to make a presentation to the local corps of prosecuting attorneys. The title selected was: "So what if the defendant's fingerprints were found on the murdered man's throat? Maybe he was just checking for a pulse."

In many jurisdictions those who compare evidence to known exemplar prints are police officers whose primary responsibilities are the protection of life and property and the apprehension of wrongdoers. Even those who are not police officers are almost always employed by police agencies. These circumstances will imply to many an automatic bias on the part of the examiner, which should not be the case. Regardless of the status of the examiner, every comparison must be an objective task; the conclusions that are expressed must be based solely upon what is observed in the examination. It is not the purpose of any comparison to identify the suspected malefactor; the purpose is to determine whether or not a particular individual is the donor of a particular print of unknown origin.

This is not to say that the examiner cannot, under any circumstances, consider factors other than the materials to be compared. The examiner may be presented with a case involving a limited population, for example, or may be asked to express an opinion regarding how an individual would have to be positioned in order to leave prints in a certain place in a certain orientation. Consideration of these factors is well within the purview of the competant examiner, but it must be made quite clear by the examiner that they were considered in arriving at whatever conclusion is expressed. Such a conclusion should also be expressed in a manner that does not exclude any other reasonable hypothesis.

In the court system in which the author works, testimony regarding the conclusions reached as the result of comparison of friction skin prints must be given by an "expert." The status of expert is determined in each case by the judge hearing the matter and is not determined by any organization or agency. Regardless of the experience or training of the witness, the court is, in every case, quite free to deny him or her the opportunity to testify. Just as an examiner with impressive credentials may be denied the opportunity to testify, one with little in the way of training and experience can be allowed to testify as an expert witness. The only requirement here is that the witness have some knowledge of the subject that exceeds common knowledge.

Any witness may testify to what he or she observed or did. The expert witness testifies to what he or she *believes* is the meaning of what was observed. Without qualifying as an expert, the examiner may testify to acts performed ("I compared the prints") and observations ("I saw numerous similarities between the two prints"). The result of what was done and what was observed is an opinion, regarding the significance of the observed similarities and is what the examiner, testifying as an expert witness, believes to be a fact. The trier of fact (the court or jury) is charged with the tasks of deciding how accurate the witness' determination may be and how significant it is to the question of guilt or innocence.

The role of the expert witness is well defined and the examiner, when testifying as an expert witness, must be cautious to not depart from that role. To do so may overemphasize the significance of the identification (or nonidentification). For instance, in settings where all of the participants are fully aware of the role of the expert witness, it may be appropriate to state that "the latent print and the inked print were made by the same individual." In other situations, such as trials before a jury, it is more appropriate to precede that statement with "it is my opinion that. . ., in so doing, the witness is observing his or her proper role in the judicial system and leaving the determination of "fact" to the triers of fact.

The final task of the examiner is to communicate the results of the examinations or comparisons that are made. These communications will invariably involve written reports and many will conclude with oral testimony in judicial proceedings. The specificity of the information communicated may vary depending upon the audience to which it is directed. A written report intended for use by investigators or prosecuting attorneys may simply state: "the latent print is identified as having been made by. . ., in this case the qualifying phrase "it is my opinion that. . ." is implied and understood by the reader. Recipients of such communications are also little interested in the justification or rationale for the conclusions expressed.

In the courtroom, however, the examiner is often asked to relate the rationale for the opinions expressed. Depending upon the requirements of the examiner's jurisdiction or, perhaps, on the preference of the examiner, comparisons are sometimes illustrated using photographic enlargements of the materials compared. In these situations it is necessary for the examiner to be articulate and convincing. It is here, however, that examiners often do their field a disservice by deemphasizing their role in reaching the expressed conclusions, presenting what they do as a simple task involving the ability to count to a certain number.

Even when the examiner must find a certain number of matching characteristics before opining that two prints share a common source, he or she must first determine whether what is seen is sufficient for the purpose of the tally. If a particular characteristic is obscured, the examiner may still, based upon experience, conclude that it is adequate. Although many comparison results are based upon easily observable characteristics, many others are determined by the skill of the examiner in "sorting out" characteristics from the effects of background and overlain prints and by the experience which allows the examiner to judge properly the significance of what is seen. An identification is not made because there are X number of similarities between two prints, but rather because a *sufficient degree of similarity* (or a sufficient number of similarities, if the examiner is so inclined) was found between the prints to convince the examiner that the two prints share a common source. In the extreme case where the examiner must find a minimum number of corresponding characteristics because of legislation or judicial fiat, it is still the examiner who determines that the minimum number of characteristics exists.

In virtually every text and article the author has read that deals with the presentation of expert testimony, the reader is cautioned against using jargon—verbal shorthand that may be used and understood by co-workers but which imparts little intelligible information to the uninitiated. An example of this would be the use of the word "points" to denote characteristic ridge formations such as ending ridges, bifurcations, and dots. Without the explanation, someone not aware of the meaning of the term would have difficulty in judging the significance of the examiner's testimony.

If one examiner were to tell another examiner that two prints were found to be identical, both would be aware that what was meant was that the two prints shared a common source. If the examiner were then to show the same two prints to a layman and describe them as identical, the layman, if as astute and argumentative as many attorneys are, might quickly point out that the prints do not really look at all alike. As in any field, terms have been coined to describe the features of friction ridges and the practices and techniques of their recording, collection, and comparison. Although this technical jargon may be necessary and useful to the performance of the task, it is unwise to redefine and use words that may be confusing to the layman because of their common use and meaning.

Dr. Paul Kirk (1963) wrote: "Criminalistics is an occupation that has all of the responsibility of medicine, the intricacy of the law, and the universality of science. Inasmuch as it carries higher penalties for error than other professions, it is not a matter to take lightly, nor to trust to luck . . .." Just as any of the fields that are ordinarily considered to fall into the realm of "criminalistics" are forensic sciences, so is that of the comparison of friction skin prints—the statement applies equally well.

There is no field in the forensic sciences that enjoys the special status of the identification of individuals by the use of the characteristics of friction skin. Popularized in literature and the media, fingerprints are "known" by the masses to be the means of certain, incontrovertible proof of identity. Courts have accepted such identifications to the extent that it is possible for an individual to be convicted of a crime with no more evidence than that his or her prints were found in a particular place or on a certain object. For this to not be the case would require the denial of the experience of a century of work in the field by untold numbers of workers. Therefore, those who would work in the field have a special responsibility.

References

Adcock, J.M. 1977. "The Development of Latent Fingerprints on Human Skin: The Iodine–Silver Plate Method." *Journal of Forensic Sciences* 22(3):599–605.

Arima, T. 1981. "Development of Latent Fingerprints on Sticky Surfaces by Dye Staining or Fluorescent Brightening." *Identification News* 31(2):9–10.

Bidloo, G. 1685. *Anatomia Humani Corporis.* Amsterdam,:Publ.

Cooke, T.D. 1973. *Fingerprint and Identification Magazine* 55(4):2 (editorial).

Cummins, H., and Kennedy, R.W. 1940. *American Journal of Criminal Law and Criminology* 31:343–356.

Cummins, H., and Midlo, C. 1961. *Finger Prints, Palms and Soles: An Introduction to Dermatolyphics.* New York: Dover, pp. 191–234.

Dalrymple, B.E., Duff, J.M., and Menzel, E.R. 1977. "Inherent Fingerprint Luminescence—Detection by Laser." *Journal of Forensic Sciences* 22:106.

Datta, P.K. 1966. "Quantitative Genetics of Plantar Main-Line Index." *Acta Geneticae Medicae et Gemellologicae* (Basel) 16:89–94.

Duff, J.M., and Menzel, E.R. 1977. "Laser-Assisted Thin-Layer Chromatography and Luminescence of Fingerprints: An Approach to Fingerprint Age Determination." *Journal of Forensic Sciences* 22:129–134.

Faulds, Henry. 1880. "On the Skin-Furrows of the Hand." *Nature* 22:605.

Federal Bureau of Investigation. 1972. "An Analysis of Standards in Fingerprint Identification." *FBI Law Enforcement Bulletin* 41(6):7–11 and 29–30.

Federal Bureau of Investigation. 1973. *The Science of Fingerprints.* Washington, D.C.: U.S. Government Printing Office, p. 191.

Galton, Francis. 1965 [1892]. *Finger Prints.* New York: Da Capo Press [orig. publ., London: MacMillan], p. 110.

Grew, Nehemiah. 1684. "The Description and Use of the Pores in the Skin of the Hands and Feet." *Philosophical Transactions of the Royal Society of London* 14:506.

Gupta, S.R. 1968. "Statistical Survey of Ridge Characteristics." *International Criminal Police Review* (218):130–134.

Gutierrez, C.H. 1978. "Developing and Photographing Latent Prints Found on Human Skin." Unpublished paper presented to the California Div., International Association for Identification, May.

Holt, S.B. 1968. *The Genetics of Dermal Ridges.* Springfield, Illinois: Charles C. Thomas, Publ.

International Association for Identification. 1973. "Report of the Standardization Committee." *Fingerprint and Identification Magazine* 55(4):11–16.

Kirk, P.L. 1963. "The Ontogeny of Criminalistics." *Journal of Criminal Law, Criminology and Police Science* 54(2):238.

Kirk, Paul. 1974. *In Crime Investigation*, 2nd ed. Thornton, J.I. (ed). New York: John Wiley and Sons, p. 71.

Larson, J.K. 1962. "The Starch Powder–Steam Method of Fixing Iodine Fumed Latent Prints." *Fingerprint and Identification Magazine* 44:3.

Malpighi, M. 1686. *De Externo Tactus Organo.* London: Publ.

Mayer, J.C.A. 1783–1788. *Anatomische Kupfertafeln nebst dazu gehörigen Erklärungen.* City: Publ. (Fingerprints described in the 1788 section.)

McLaughery, R.W. 1896. *The Bertillon System of Identification.* Chicago: McLaughery.

Mehta, M.K. 1963. *The Identification of Thumb Impressions and the Cross Examination of Finger Print Experts.* Bombay: N.M. Tripathi Private, Ltd., p. 30.

Mitsui, T., Katho, H., Shimada, K., and Wagasugi, Y. 1980. "Development of Latent Prints Using a Sudan Black-B Solution." *Identification News* 30(8):9–10.

Moenssens, A.A. 1969. *Fingerprints and the Law.* Philadelphia: Chilton Book Co., p. 27.

Moenssens, A.A. 1970. *Fingerprint Techniques.* Philadelphia: Chilton Book Co.

Montagna, W. 1956. *The Structure and Function of Skin.* New York: Academic Press, pp. 89, 255, 263.

Mukherjee, D.P. 1966. "Inheritance of the Total Number of Triradii on Fingers, Palms and Soles." *Annual of Human Genetics, London* (29):349.

Nariyuki, H., Ueda, K., and Sasaki, T. 1971. "A New Method for the Detection of Bloody Latent Fingerprints." *Fingerprint and Identification Magazine* 52(12):3–5.

Olsen, R.D. 1978. *Scotts Fingerprint Mechanics.* Springfield, Illinois: Charles C. Thomas, Publ.

Osterburg, J.W., Parthasarathy, T., Raghavan, T., and Sclove, S.L. 1977. "Development of a Mathematical Formula for the Calculation of Fingerprint Probabilities Based on Individual Characteristics." *Journal of the American Statistical Association.* 72(360):772–778.

Purkinje, J.E. 1823. *Commentatio de Examine Physiologico Organi Visus et Systematis Cutanei.* Breslau: Publ. [See Cummins and Kennedy (1940).]

Reed, F. 1980–1981. "Fingermark Recovery—An Outline of Some Current Reagents and a Look to the Future." *Police Research Bulletin* (35,36):32–38.

Srivastava, R.P. 1965. "A Quantitative Analysis of the Fingerprints of the Tharsus of Uttar Pradesh." *American Journal of Physical Anthropology, N.S.* 23(2):pp. 99–106.

Stone, R.S., and Metzger, R.A. 1981. "Comparison of Development Techniques for Water-Soaked Porous Items." *Identification News* 31(1):13, 14.

Trowell, F. 1975. "A Method for Fixing Latent Fingerprints Developed with Iodine." *Journal of the Forensic Science Society* 15:189.

Index